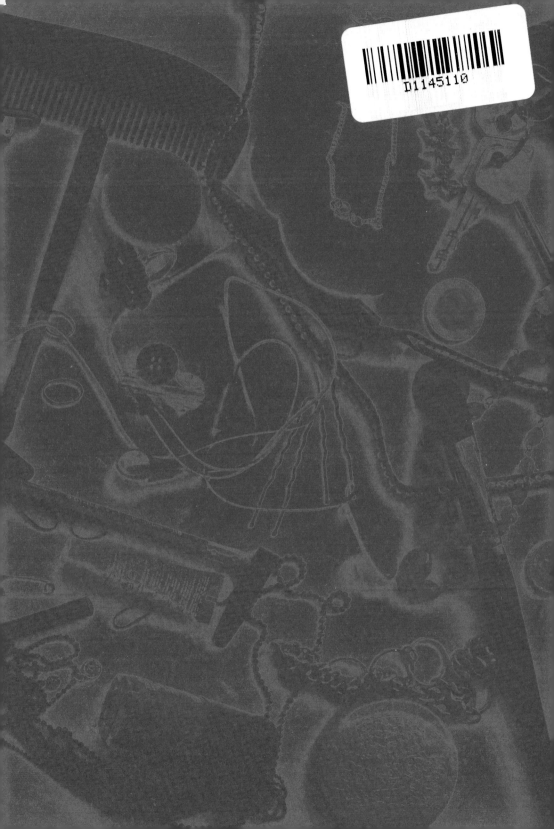

The Best Friends' Guide to Life

10 9 8 7 6 5 4 3 2 1

Published in 2010 by Vermilion, an imprint of Ebury Publishing

A Random House Group Company

The Random House Group Limited Reg. No. 954009

Addresses for companies within the Random House Group can be found at www.randomhouse.co.uk

A CIP catalogue record for this book is available from the British Library

The Random House Group Limited supports The Forest Stewardship Council (FSC), the leading international forest certification organisation. All our titles that are printed on Greenpeace approved FSC-certified paper carry the FSC logo. Our paper procurement policy can be found at www.rbooks.co.uk/environment

Printed and bound by Firmengruppe APPL, Aprinta Druck, Wemding, Germany
Inside design Dave Brown © Ape Inc. Ltd 2010
Illustration © Ivana Zorn 2010
Additional illustration © Fearne Cotton 2010

9780091935405

To buy books by your favourite authors and register for offers visit www.rbooks.co.uk

The Best Friends' Guide to Life

Fearne Cotton & Holly Willoughby

Vermilion

DEDICATION

FEARNE: To Linda, Sylvia and Ruby. Three very different women who have shown me what being a woman is all about.

HOLLY: To Dan, for making the fairy tale come true . . . I love you.

Contents

LIFE IS LIKE A CAKE AND EACH OF THE SLICES REPRESENTS A PART OF THE WHOLE. THE REAL PROBLEM IS KEEPING THEM ALL IN BALANCE SO THAT THE WORK SLICE DOESN'T TAKE OVER FROM THE FAMILY SLICE OR THE FRIENDS' SLICE. WE ARE ALL SEARCHING FOR THE RIGHT BALANCE – AND THE CHERRY ON TOP THAT MAKES LIFE PERFECT.

FEARNE COTTON – ANNIE'S RESTAURANT, LONDON, 2009

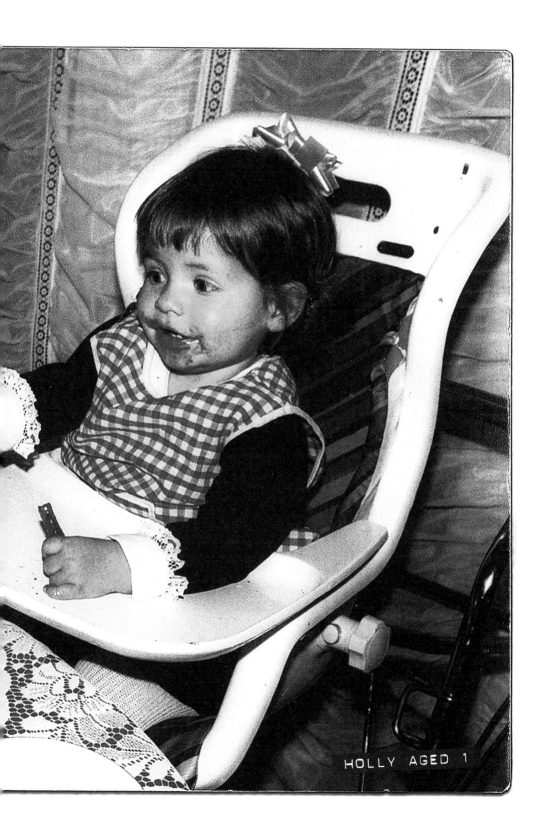

HOLLY AGED 1

This is the first book that either of us has written and we really hope you love it as much as we do! This is definitely not one of those bossy manuals that tells you how to live your life: how to jog on the spot, put your legs behind your ears, live on fresh air and a lettuce leaf and be happy while you are doing it. Nor is it one of those showing-off celebrity books that tells how you marvellous the author is while they advise you on where to buy super-expensive shoes, skin-tight dresses and how often you need to massage your thighs! This is a book written by proper best friends who have been working together and journeying together for over ten years. We have written it for our mates, peers, pals and contemporaries and in it we hope we can share a few things, tips and ideas that we have picked up on our way. We are not telling you how to do anything! But we have made many mistakes and learnt quite a few lessons and we hope that by sharing them with you we might help you a bit on your own journey. We also hope that, while being helpful, this book might make you laugh, entertain you, touch you and most of all that it might become a bit like talking to your very best friend. So crack open the biscuits, find yourself a nice comfortable sofa, curl up and enjoy!

Loads of love from us both,

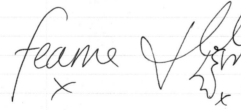

P.S. Throughout the book each of us comment, give our opinion and chat to each other about certain subjects. The following key lets you know who's talking when.

 = Holly, = Fearne.

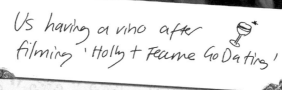

Us having a vino after filming 'Holly + Fearne Go Dating'

When cutting up your cake of life, it is very tempting to make this slice the biggest, boldest, bestest slice of all. After all, your mates are certainly one of the most important things in your life! They make you happy, they get you drunk, they keep you sane and they pick up the pieces when it all goes wrong.

And unlike your family, who were foisted on you at birth, you get to choose your mates. And hopefully you have made some good choices. The one who loves you, the one who teaches you stuff, the one who leads you astray, the one who makes you laugh. There are bound to be a few duds in there, because we all have a few of those. The ones you're not quite sure why you love, but love them you do. They are all important, crucial even, and we think if you had asked both of us to cut a mates' slice a few years ago it might well have been over half the cake. But we are a tiny bit older now and there are quite a lot of elements jostling for our attention so we are trying to keep them in proportion. That is not to say they aren't important, because they are. Particularly our best mates – each other.

*Us (hungover) on Santa Monica
Girls Holiday* ☼

We were about 19 or 20 when we met and we just clicked. And you just know at that age, as you kind of know yourself a bit by then, and we were at the same stage in our lives. We were both just beginning to do stuff, our careers were taking off, we were both presenting children's TV and we were both excited about work.

It was like we were both singing from the same hymn sheet. We liked talking about the same things. We liked talking about boys, clothes and what we were going to drink next.

Sarah Cawood, a fellow TV presenter, introduced us at CBBC. We then spent the next two years in each other's pockets. We went on holiday together. We went out drinking together. And like most best friends there is not one particular moment when it works; you just find that you fit together. Your interests may be different but fundamentally the same things make you laugh and the same things make you cry.

F *Holly is my first port of call when it comes to me being dumped or dumping. My poor mother can't take any more, so I either ring Hols or my great mate Kye, he is a bloke so I always get a different perspective from him. Holly has been through all my boyfriend problems. She is totally brilliant at coming over and staying up late on the sofa with a bottle of wine. Or two.*

H *Fearne's never really had to scoop me up off the floor after a bloke problem because I've always been kind of settled since I met her. But she is a great mate in a crisis. I do remember the two of us being stuck in Hull during the floods while we were shooting our dating show (Holly and Fearne Go Dating) and I couldn't make the final fitting of my wedding dress. I was in pieces panicking about the thing not fitting properly on the big day and she just kept me sane. I think we watched seven episodes of Sex and The City while we crawled home in the back of the car and all I could think of was my dress, while the people of Hull were slowly drowning!*

That is not to say that best mates don't drive you nuts or have their own teeniest tiniest faults!

H *Fearne's phobia of her phone drives me mad! She never picks it up to call and she never answers it when it rings. All she ever wants to do is text and I have the texting speed of a 70-year-old gran so I can't keep up and it drives me bonkers. Pick up the phone, Fearne! Have a conversation and be done with it!*

F *Holly's life is just so settled and sorted with her nice house, her husband, her baby and her plumped cushions, all I can think of whenever I come back to my house after I have spent some time with her is that I must grow up. Note to self: Fearne, get yourself a little bit more organised and stop living like a student.*

H *Really? I love that I've created such a façade! Under the plumped cushions there's always a crushed packet of biscuits and a cork from last night's wine.*

HOW FAR ARE YOU REALLY ALLOWED TO GO WHEN TALKING TO YOUR MATES? THE TRUTH? THE WHOLE TRUTH? OR JUST HALFWAY THERE?

We have all been there. Your friend asks for your opinion, they want your advice. Does my backside look big in these electric-pink hot pants? Should I go out with my best mate's brother? Was I really badly behaved last night? What you have to judge is exactly how truthful they really want you to be. Are you being cruel to be kind or just plain cruel? The answers are probably: the pink hot pants are terrible. The best mate's brother is toxic. And no, you were fine – everyone loved the pole dance!

F *Holly is probably the only one I would accept total honesty from and not be offended. I know she is saying it because she is my best mate and she loves me.*

H *I try to be totally honest. I am not hiding things from you. There are, however, ways of saying things. If it is a sensitive issue, you can't just go gung-ho. You have to use all your diplomacy and tact and be very aware where you tread.*

F *You do kind of know when you've overstepped the mark. I am caught between two mates at the moment and I was a little bit too honest with one of them the other night and all that happened is she more or less shut up shop. But it is what being friends is all about. Being totally honest and saying what you feel. There is nothing worse than having an elephant in the room or a whole load of tension.*

TABOO SUBJECTS

No matter how honest and open we feel our friendships are, no matter how much we love our friends and think we have their best interests at heart, there are some subjects that are definitely off-limits. Anything that involves family. So, 'your mother is ugly'; 'your brother is a git'; 'your sister is a loser' are all no-nos. As is the current squeeze, so 'your boyfriend has a huge backside' is just not worth sharing. Also totally honest appraisals of their work are not the best things to get off your chest at 3 am after a bottle and a half of white wine.

F *There are some things I just wouldn't comment on, like friends' parents, their relationships or their weight. Holly has in the past told me a few home truth about ex-boyfriends of mine that have been brutally honest and I have been a bit taken aback and a bit: 'OK, that's a lot for me to take on board.' But in the end it probably made me think.*

H *It is important to watch what you say to your mates. A bit of honesty goes a long way – just be careful it doesn't go too far!*

HOW MANY MATES DO YOU NEED?

You are, so researchers say, supposed to have 18 friends in your lifetime. Some you pick up early and apparently stay forever. Others are like shooting stars that burn brightly in your firmament only to disappear as quickly as they came. Others stay around well past their sell-by dates and, like fish or guests at Christmas, go rotten after three days. One thing we both know is the older you get, the sad truth is the less time you have for your mates, and indeed the less time they have for you. Our lives become overloaded with other commitments, so we can't spend all afternoon listening to a friend play drums down the phone, or spend all day watching TV together or even meet up for a wine and a whine at a moment's notice. It's one of life's harder realities.

F *My mates' level has definitely shrunk. When I was younger, I was happy to spend fleeting moments with anyone just so long as I was having a laugh. But my capacity to make new mates has definitely reduced.*

Me, charlie and Becky AKA BABS
AKA Curriehead DJing in Sheffield!

H *I'm glad mine has. I just don't have time any more for that many mates. Between seeing Dan and my family and having a baby – there is not much time to spend with the close friends I have already. So I would say I have probably got about ten really close friends.*

F *I have a few more, about 20 close mates. And then about 100 other mates who I would have to a big old Christmas party. When people say you don't make friends in later life, I think that's wrong. I have had some really key people pop into my life almost by accident. But they have to be special, almost like you have been looking for them all your life.*

H *If you make a friend now, it is not like the mates you made earlier in life. If you are going to put the energy in, there has to be a real reason.*

So now we think it is the quality of your mates rather than the quantity of them that makes the difference. Instead of adding to your collection for the sake of it, you should perhaps enjoy the mates you have, and make sure you look after them.

F It is so hard trying to keep up with everyone and give people the amount of attention they deserve, but I do try and I do prioritise. I had some acquaintance get really stroppy with me the other day because I couldn't find time to see them. I had not seen my mum or my old mates, but they kept on asking to meet up. Eventually I said I could make something in three weeks' time and I got this harsh text back saying: 'I am beginning to think that we are never going to meet up and you are never going to commit to anything. I thought we were friends? I invited you to my party before Xmas and you never replied. This is very hurtful.' I have to say, I was stunned. Close mates don't put pressure on you. You can dump them at the last minute if you have to and they still love you because they understand. You don't see them for weeks and it doesn't matter, you just pick up where you left off the next time you do see them.

H I can be quite guilty of being friend-lazy as well. Because I work quite hard, the last thing I want to do is get on the phone and start organising things. It is awful and sometimes I think you need to sit down and make the effort. Sometimes I have dragged myself somewhere reluctantly and then I've had a really good time and I have had to have a little word with myself about making the effort more often. It is all about balance.

HOW TO BE A BEST MATE

We all like to think of ourselves as good friends. You're the sort of person who is consistently reliable and always there for your mate. But quite often this is not the case. Being a 'best' friend takes practice and requires a certain amount of concentration. It is very easy, particularly if things are going well for you, to get caught up in your own life. With your head up, you aim for the horizon, your bags packed, and you don't check in with your mates, you don't return their calls and when you do you don't really listen to what they are saying. Often it is the stuff that remains unsaid that's the most important of all. It's the silences you have to really listen to.

Never underestimate the brilliance of a very close friend, and you have to treat them accordingly. You have to be on the end of the phone any time of the day or night.

There are certain things that are a given. You have to remember birthdays. Take their call at midnight. Lend them money for a taxi to get home and never ask for it back.

Time is also the biggest thing you can give a friend. Listening to them and being relaxed with them.

Because, in the end, we all know what it is like to be let down, to feel that the traffic is one way, to feel unloved and un-nurtured, to be taken for granted.

I had a close friend who left the school we were at to go to some posh school – never to be seen again. We were supposed to throw a leaving party for her when she went travelling – we did, and she never showed up. Not to her own party! It was like we were not good enough for her any more, despite the fact we had all grown up together. Some years later, I moved to London and thought, well, that was that. And then the moment I started to be on the telly – my phone was red-hot. She called and called me. And I have never replied to her. She still texts me occasionally and I just don't reply to her but still she persists. It was really hurtful. Now I am apparently good enough to be back in her life. But I won't forget the years that I wasn't.

Different

TYPES

O F

FRIEND

Over the years we have noticed that there are certain friends you always end up doing certain things with. You have friends you go out drinking with. Friends you stay and watch TV with. Friends you go on holiday with. Mates you go to gigs with, go clubbing with, take home to see your mum. There are mates you trust when it comes to talking about boyfriends. Mates you will take shopping when you want to shell out on a killer dress. There are mates whose advice you seek when it comes to your career. Occasionally there will be a crossover – the drinking mate is also the career mate, or the stylist mate is the one you take home to see your mum. But often the worst offenders fall into set categories like these!

The Princess Friend

We have all suffered at the hands of the Princess Pal. This is the person who calls the shots and, much like Veruca Salt in *Charlie and the Chocolate Factory*, she wants everything, and that is EVERYTHING, her own way. The day/evening out/holiday is entirely on her terms. So you find yourself driving across town to a place you don't want to be at, doing something you don't want to do and most likely paying for the both of you. Princesses don't carry cash and most obviously Princesses don't carry their own bags. Both of us have ended up struggling through the airport carrying girlfriends' bags as well as our own. Princesses are extraordinarily manipulative and through the use of some very clever passive-aggressive behaviour, they always manage to make you do all the crappy stuff, while they just simply look the other way.

HOLLY

27

HOLLY AND SISTER

28

H I had a mate who wouldn't buy loo roll because she wouldn't walk down the street carrying the stuff and she wouldn't tidy up, either. I remember always being the one cleaning everything and going back and forth to the shops with a big pack of Andrex under my arm as she walked four steps behind me, pretending I didn't exist.

F I used to work with a girl who was cheating on her boyfriend and she used to use my flat as a knocking shop and use my phone to talk to the other boyfriend. It took me ages to realise I was being used and then our friendship steadily dwindled. I am not very good at saying no. I did have another mate who was completely diva-ish. We were working together, and instead of her being part of the team, I had to look after her the whole time. I had to make sure she had enough to eat, talk constantly about her love life, and all the time I was supposed to be working and learning my lines for the show. She wanted my full-time attention. It was exhausting.

Bullyboy Mates

If being with a Princess is like trying to indulge the wishes and whims of a six-year-old child high on Jelly Tots, then dealing with Bullyboy Mates is a little bit more intimidating. Instead of being guilt-tripped into something by a pouting lip or hair flick or out of fear of hurting your friend's feelings – with a Bullyboy Mate you are forced into a corner you can't get out of. You try and politely extricate yourself from the scenario, or tactfully take a step back. You avoid their calls, you try and slip away from their emails but they just won't take the hint. Short of shouting 'No!' directly into their ear, they just don't seem to listen.

F I try to cut people out of my life who aren't good for me. When I was younger I was keen on impressing people but now I don't care. But I did have a friend who was really emotionally demanding and would tell me things I didn't want to hear, and she would try and make us appear as a cool gang to the outside world, which is not my style. So she would be very bitchy and private-jokey in front of other people. And I would overcompensate, because I am a people-pleaser. Then she ended up asking me for stuff all the time in front of other people, bullying me, and I would always say yes. It was awful.

H Some people just don't get the hint. You have been polite and kind and tried tactfully to say you are busy and then they call up and say: 'How about June?' It is almost impossible to find a way out of that conversation without being rude. I have worked out the best thing is to say: 'I don't know, I will have to look in my diary', and leave it at that. Otherwise you just end up being unkind and no-one wants that.

The Offloader

We are all quite capable of doing this. In fact, truth be known, both of us are really rather good at talking about ourselves for hours at a time. Often to each other. But good friends know there is a sort of protocol you have to follow for a friendship, or indeed even a dinner or telephone conversation, to work. One person tells a story while the other one listens. The first person gets a certain amount of air time while the second person nods, sympathises, possibly empathises, gasps when she needs to gasp and then attempts to ask the appropriate questions, the answers to which, conversational law dictates, she must also listen to. Then the whole process is reversed. A night out with an Offloader, however, is entirely different. They open their mouths, dump all their rubbish on you and then go home significantly lighter. Meanwhile you sit there with your rubbish still festering, while at the same time having to deal with theirs. It is not a good night out and you end up feeling sullied and cheated in some way.

F *I have one friend who just rings and complains, then when I mention something, she announces she's got to go! It is really annoying.*

However, as a good friend you are allowed the occasional offloading night. If you have been dumped, have a career crisis or had a bad fight with a mate, then a certain amount of offloading is allowed. You can monopolise the conversation for a while, but then it is time to call it quits.

F *I am the first to admit I am quite capable of talking about boys and work till the cows come home but I did have a mate who would not stop talking about the same thing the whole time over and over, and eventually I turned round and said: 'OK, your love life. You have until eight o'clock and then we are not allowed to talk about it again.' It worked. I listened because I knew I didn't have to talk about the same thing the whole night, and she got to share her stuff before we talked about something else. It's the only way to deal with it.*

The Talented Miss Ripley

Otherwise known as the Single White Female or the Stalker, the Miss Ripley is the ultimate competitive friend who slowly but surely takes over you and your life. She starts to wear the same clothes as you, she hangs out in the same places as you, she tries to steal your other friends, she takes an interest in the same things as you and in the end she morphs into you and starts sounding like you on the telephone, using the same words and vocabulary. We have one friend whose Miss Ripley friend tried on her wedding dress while she was looking at veils in the shop. It freaked out the shop assistant so much that she had to ask who was the bride. Some Miss Ripley friends are benign – they just like you so much they want to be like you. Others are a little more extreme and want to take over your life. It's the extreme Ripleys that are worrying.

F I had a close mate who took on the identity of people around her. She changed career to mirror mine. She got obsessed with the guy I was dating. Anything I liked, she liked too. It got kind of scary. The only thing to do in that situation is to withdraw and stop allowing that person into your life. Take a million steps back and hopefully they won't turn up at the same pub as you in the same clothes.

H Talking of which, I was working with another female presenter a while back who would go out and buy exactly the same outfits as mine and wear them to work. It got so bad that one day I went to get a car home from work and the cab controller called me the name of the other girl. We had finally morphed into one!

Obviously not all our mates have some sort of mad crazy foible or quirk that we tolerate – or indeed not tolerate – because we like them. There are others who are easier to love and even some who enhance our lives beyond compare.

Little Miss Stylish

She's the girl who looks good in something slinky and second-hand from Oxfam. She has a natural eye, and can mix and match old and new, cheap and expensive, and always look fantastic. And she is the only mate you should ever go shopping with.

H I have a very good mate, Jo, who sometimes goes shopping for me. She has a good eye and she is brilliant in that she takes me out of my comfort zone, because I am always buying the same old stuff just in different colours. The other day she turned up with a whole load of amazing clothes: cute little jackets, that sort of thing. Stuff I would never buy. I did draw the line at the harem pants, though; they were a step too far! But she is incredible. Every girl should have a friend like her.

My friend India is one of the best shoppers on the planet. She does GREAT shopping, just the way I like it. QUICK. We can supermarket-sweep the high street in minutes and come out with bargains galore. She sometimes does Portobello, which is fun, and she's always tipping me off about great new websites. I trust her with style 100 per cent, and recently before the NME awards she actually went out and got my whole outfit for me, without me even seeing it, hours before the awards. She has a great eye and is the perfect shopping buddy. She is also one of the best cupcake-makers around, which makes for great post-shopping relief.

Party Pals

As well as the friends you drink tea with, go for long walks with and take home to your mum, there are also friends you go drinking with, who get you into trouble, who lead you astray. They pick you up when you are down, they help you celebrate when you are up and they're an instant party on the end of the phone.

H I have a friend, Mel, who is always out; she loves being out. She is never in watching Corrie on the sofa. She is a very important friend to me and whenever I want to go out and let off steam, she's the one I call. Although I have to say, I am hardly falling out of China Whites – we go out and have dinner and a couple of bottles of wine. But Dan and I entertain a lot more at home these days, mainly because Harry is asleep upstairs.

F I have a gang of mates called Team Mayhem, born from a night out when I DJ'd at a club in Essex called Mayhem. They are Becky (aka Currie Head; her surname is Currie), Kye (bezzie) and Bundy. We had a riot in the car on the way, and partied hard while we were there. At one point I had to have them removed from the DJ booth as they were causing such chaos – throwing glowsticks about and bashing into my decks. We made it back to mine in one piece and crashed out. The next morning we lay around my kitchen recalling tales of the previous night's escapades. They know exactly how to pick me up when I'm not in the partying mood and give me the energy and laughs I need for a night out.

Culture Vulture

Everyone needs a mate who stretches their mind, makes them think a little harder and challenges their everyday ideas about things. Often the night out or away day seems a terrible idea and you drag yourself there thinking miserable thoughts. But at the end of it all you come home refreshed, excited and totally delighted you went.

F *I feel lucky that a lot of my mates have the same passions as me. I have many friends who are up for browsing a museum or gallery without complaining their feet hurt or they're bored. Kye is the music king so we, along with his flatmate Smithy, gig a lot and see new bands and enjoy the music scene together. My mate Hayley is an exceptional artist and puts my paintings to shame. We used to go to galleries a lot when we were younger and even once visited Paris to go to as many galleries in one weekend as possible. We can chat about Toulouse-Lautrec and Jenny Saville for hours. While in Paris we got mugged, which made for a detour on our weekend of culture as we ended up in a French police station using broken French to describe the man who stole our money. This resulted in a what-the-hell attitude that led to us having an amazing night out in a swanky French nightclub we managed to blag our way into. We got bought champs all night long by a group of men who believed our mad story that we were fashion buyers from London who had a shop called KARMA in Carnaby Street! We now have matching (slightly tragic) tattoos on our hips that say 'KARMA'.*

H *I have a friend called Neil who always does the most weird and wonderful things. He always has tickets to things and has lots of ideas. The other day he asked a girlfriend of mine out for the day. She had to think of a number between one and fifteen, and then another number between one and fifteen. He then took her to Victoria Station. The first number was the platform they stood on to catch the train. The second number was the station they had to get off at. They then went into that town, had a fabulous pub lunch and explored.*

TROUBLESHOOTING YOUR FRIENDS

Even your loveliest friends can cause you problems. We have both lost count of the amount of times we have been dumped, ditched, dropped or just plain sent to Coventry by our nearest and dearest. Sometimes it is genuinely our fault – a tactless comment here, saying something silly we should not have said, or we have simply let someone down when we didn't mean to. And sometimes it is not our fault at all. But good friends are hard to come by and a good mixture of mates is important. Nights out with your Drinking and Style mates are a huge laugh, and even Miss Ripley can be fun once in a while. The toxic Bullyboy ones are to be avoided and lanced like boils as soon as possible, obviously. But the others we try to hold on to, as hard as we can. We always try to make amends if we have screwed up. But some situations can make it quite difficult . . .

KEEPING MALE MATES WHEN YOU ARE MARRIED OR IN A RELATIONSHIP

It happens all the time. Your great friend gets a boyfriend and you don't see her for dust. Or at least for a few months, but she usually bounces back wanting to go out on a girls' night or discuss her recent break-up. But if you are a bloke, it is much worse. Your friend, who happens to be a girl, gets a boyfriend and you are often kicked into touch for good.

An ex of mine had real problems with me having close male friends. He kept on saying: 'I don't believe it. What are you doing? Why are you talking to him?' And I would say: 'Because he is a big girl and I love him and I want to talk to him.' But it made the whole situation very difficult. Fortunately Dan, my husband, is not like that. But you can see it causing terrible problems in relationships and what it boils down to in the end is who you think is the most important.

F *If the bloke is a real lad type, then he tends not to understand your need for platonic male friends. 'Lads' can't understand how you can have a male friend who is just a mate. Equally I have one best male mate who always passes judgement on my boyfriends, which is hard, too, because I trust his judgement and he doesn't say things lightly; he only says things out of concern for me.*

The thing is that most blokes don't realise there are boyfriends you marry and then there are male friends you go and have a drink with, male friends you have known all your life who you adore. There are male friends you flirt with, male friends who put a spring in your stride, for whom you might put on your sexiest dress but you have no intention of ever sleeping with. Just as there are horses for courses, so there are different boys for different occasions and you don't want to snog or sleep with any of them!

Kye (best mate) and Holly at my 50's night house party!

H I think if you are introducing a male friend to your partner, it is all about how you describe them. Don't say: 'Oh you will really LOVE him.' If you big them up too much they'll hate them before they've met them.

F That's true. Then they're an instant threat. Be really low-key about the whole thing.

H Say something like: 'He is quite nice, I hope you like him.' If you go on and on about how great they are, it will have the opposite effect. You have to let them get to know and like each other first and then cross your fingers that it works.

F There is nothing sadder than having a boyfriend and a best mate who don't get on. But you should not dump the best mate for the boyfriend, as mates last forever and often boyfriends don't get beyond Christmas!

KEEPING IN TOUCH WITH PEOPLE YOU GREW UP WITH

Life is indeed all about balance and trying to be true to yourself while at the same time challenging yourself and chasing your dreams. Neither of us now lives in the places we were born in. Work has made us come to the capital and this means we have both left behind some good mates along the way.

H I have a handful of friends I grew up with and they are very precious to me as it is rare to keep these friends into adulthood.

F I have loads; my great mate Becky is a mate from childhood. There are about five of us who are a gang I went to school with. But then you have others, like Holly, who you meet at work. You have to make the effort with people you have known for years. Then, every now and then, you have to do a bit of life laundry and sort through the people who have just managed to cling on for some reason. You have to shut off from people you just partied with for a few years and keep the important ones.

Gravesy, Tommo and I at the Killers

Hayley, Lucy, Me, Ally AKA camholio.
Last day of school before Christmas.

𝒽 *And I don't think you should feel guilty about that. You change and move on and so do they. They are probably just as busy and have their own thing going on.*

𝓕 *I just think you need to be honest. I think you should be honest. But I am terrible at that. I am always saying: 'Yeah, yeah, let's meet up'. And I have no intention of ever doing it!*

YOUR SIM CARD IS FULL

There are just not enough hours in the day to be nice to all the people all the time, so you are entitled to be picky and choosy. Better to be a good friend to a few than an average friend to many.

𝓕 *You have a certain amount of space for a certain amount of people.*

𝒽 *It depends what sort of relationship you are in as to how much you need your mates around. If your man is very blokey you tend to need your mates more to discuss things. My husband is pretty good at talking so he is like the biggest cheese in the pie – he has bumped off about ten people!*

OOOHHH! I COULDN'T EAT ANOTHER THING!

FACEBOOK FRIENDS VS FRIENDS?

Even as little as five years ago the way we socialised was different. We had a few friends we emailed, telephoned or texted, but most of our mates we got to speak to or touch in the flesh every once in a while. These days, however, you can have whole groups or gangs of mates you have never spoken to, had a drink with or even met at all. While there is a lot of fun and games and indeed sharing of gossip and information to be had sitting at a desk, typing away (both of us are avid fans of Twitter and we are always posting tweets or checking our pages), we are also convinced that nothing really beats a good night out, or even a good night in on the sofa, with your closest friends.

I have a personal Facebook for people I know and I have mates I talk to daily on there. But there are some people I was at school with, who I can't NOT 'accept', because they will think I'm a tosser. It is an awkward situation because I'm interacting with people I know I won't see again, but I don't want to be unpleasant. But it is not an environment where you can really truly be yourself. Also, because you are writing things down, there are so many things that can be taken out of context.

I am not that technical. Fearne records music off the radio for her phone and I can't even download.

That's tragic.

I know. But it's not the way I like to communicate very much. I use things like Twitter mainly for work, but I prefer talking to people. I don't even like texting that much.

It isn't that discriminating, either. You have reasons for certain friends. If you want to have a right old bitch you might go and see this person. If I want to have drink and a muck around, I might go and see Jake. Or if I want to have a quiet time I might hang out with Lolly, Holly or Kye; I can sit in silence with them.

WHAT HAPPENS WHEN YOUR MATE GOES OUT WITH OR MARRIES SOMEONE YOU DON'T LIKE?

This is one of the worst situations. It is so easy to make a mistake that ends in tears. We all know that love is blind and everyone is entitled to fall for whoever they please, but there are limits to that blindness. Part of you wants to speak your mind, part of you wants to tear the scales from their myopic eyes and say, 'Look, he's just terrible!' And the other part of you worries that if you do, it can end up in a situation where you're the one left out in the cold. We both have a friend who celebrated a friend's break-up from her boyfriend with a drunken 'He's ditched' dance only to be left off their wedding invitation list three months later. You have to play your cards carefully and very close to your chest.

F I would try and bring it up and say something but if they get married there is nothing you can do. There is a point when it's no longer your business.

H I have only stepped in once before; the guy was abusive and mean. She didn't thank me for it at the time but now she does.

F I have been the one with the bad boy and it was a nightmare. He was doing any drug he could get his hands on and I don't do anything like that at all. He had a nocturnal life. I went to work and he stayed up all night doing drugs. Most of my mates buggered off. A few stuck around and one really hung on in there and told me to get the hell out. She was honest and very strong. It took me a year to get rid of him. I was in a weird bubble and couldn't get out. So I really thank those people who did get involved. You have to go through it in your own time but you are thankful for those people who do stick it out.

Equally we should all be careful about how we talk about the people we are going out with. If all you ever do is complain about how mean and nasty your partner is, then your friends will only ever have a mean and nasty impression of him. They will only know what you tell them. So if you sit and bitch about your boyfriend when you have dumped him and then go back out with him a few months later, you have to cut your mates a bit of slack, just as you hope they'll do for you. Things once said can't be unsaid, but they can be tactfully ignored.

F *That has happened to me a few times, as I have gone back out with boys I have dumped or broken up with before. And it is hard because lots of people have said things in the past, especially my mother. We all say things in the heat of the moment, but I would rather they were there when I was pissed off with the boyfriend and giving me solace than being tactful and avoiding the whole thing. And if we end up back together then as mates they just have to deal with it. That is all part of the complexities of relationships. But recently I have learnt to talk a little less about my boyfriends. You can end up saying too much and sharing too much and then you only have yourself to blame if your mother doesn't approve of you going back out with him. Or your best mate is not keen on you going over old ground.*

CAN YOU MIX COUPLES? IS DOUBLE-DATING A GOOD IDEA?

It is one of those perfect fantasy things you only ever really see in the movies or in sit-coms like *Friends*. Everyone gets on so well that they 'double-date', going out to dinner, films or concerts together. The blokes bond and joke and talk about beer and football, and the girls joke and talk about wine and shoes. But in our experience it almost never happens.

H *There is nothing worse than your partner sitting there bored with a mate's other half. They start getting their Blackberries out and you sit there thinking, but we are out? It is Sunday lunch? What the hell are you doing? It is so rude.*

F *Very occasionally we have managed to find a couple of boys who don't mind seeing each other for an hour or so of an evening. Who will put up with each other over a bottle of wine and a pizza. But it is rare as rocking-horse poop.*

H *It has worked once for me. My last boyfriend was best mates with one of my best mate's boyfriends. We had the best time ever. They have a baby now but we still manage to have the best time. When it works, it's brilliant. You all love each other and it's fantastic.*

ANNOYING THE PANTS OFF YOU? OR BORING YOU WITLESS?

Ever had a friend you love to pieces but who is like some cracked record, whose behaviour is so repetitive and dull you almost can't even begin to go there? The same old rubbish boyfriends? The same old crying over the same problems at work? The same old going out and getting drunk and coming home with another unsuitable bloke? Week in, week out. You workshop those very same problems. How not to spend too much on credit cards. How not to get drunk and sleep with unsuitable boys. And quite frankly at the end of it all you are hoarse from giving advice and they go off and repeat the behaviour all over again.

F *To be honest, I'm sure I am the friend everyone gives the same advice to, who makes the same mistakes over and over again. I am the person who is always going out with the rubbish boyfriends, picking the same old men, dumping them or getting dumped and then going back for more!*

H *She is, and she never listens! You can say it as much as you want to Fearne but she needs to make the mistake herself. She knows what she should be doing but she just doesn't want to do it – so with the best will in the world, if she doesn't want to do it she won't. All I need to be there for is the fallout afterwards.*

F Friends like that are vital.

H I will always say it – I just don't want to keep saying it over and over again. But she always gets there in the end. Eventually.

THE MANNERS OF FRIENDS

Weirdly we think the older we get, the more we expect from our mates. Gone are the days when it was fine to sleep on our sofas, eat everything out of our fridge and leave without saying thank you. Life, so we now realise, is just too damn short to be treated badly and have mates who take the mick. Although there are certain bad habits, such as nail picking or gross flatulence, that a best friend, rather like your mum, can learn to love, there are some things you just shouldn't take. There are enough people in the world who are unpleasant and mean and rude without adding a supposedly close friend to the list.

F I am obsessed with manners. I wish people would say sorry when they bash into me in the supermarket, or would let me out of my road when I am driving. But we live in a fast-paced world where no one looks out for anyone else.

H I just like people to be polite and not be rude.

F I hate people being late. I have a mate and he's always over an hour late.

H I don't know why you take that. I'd leave. What he is saying is that his life is more important than yours.

F He always comes in saying: 'You know what I am like' and all that. Yes, I do, which is why I expect you to make an effort. Just be on time – it is not that difficult.

H I find disloyalty unforgivable. If someone says anything about Dan I find myself getting very upset. I am very protective about him. The only person who can be rude about him is me! I am also not that good about being told how to do things. If I have asked, fine, but if I haven't asked I can't abide it. I hate being patronised more than anything else!

HERMIT PHASE

Sometimes you just don't fancy seeing anyone. Sometimes you might actually just want to enjoy your own company. You'd prefer to stay in, be chilled and on your own, doing not very much. This is all fine and dandy and delightful if it doesn't become too much of a habit. It is amazing how easily a few nights in can turn a social butterfly into an antisocial couch potato with a virulent pizza habit and a propensity to watch old reruns of *Friends* – so beware!

F *I am so knackered these days, I would happily never go out again, so my friends are a good influence in that they make me go out. I did have mates back in the day who were a terrible influence, who would make me go clubbing all night and then I'd have to go straight to work. There was a time when you couldn't stop me from going out. I would say yes to anything. A gig, a drink, a club – it was mainly to meet boys! That was my incentive. But now I have to be very much persuaded to go anywhere as I have to be up early and together for my radio show.*

H *I agree, but you go though phases. I couldn't wait to have a big old blow-out after the baby was born – I needed to, I could feel it in my bones. I definitely have friends who are real party people and I also have people who make me behave and stay at home. And I call whoever I feel I need to at the time. If you are in a relationship it is hard to get your arse off the sofa; if you are single, the incentive is there.*

F *I admit, I am terrible. I have had some fantastic nights out with my girlfriends getting drunk but sometimes it is hard to stop yourself thinking, what is the end result of this? Me feeling rubbish the next day – when before it was a possible snog! Although, actually, it is always good to know what's out there!*

H *But you should enjoy your girlfriends and make the effort. You never know when you might need them and if you do make the effort you get it back times ten, every time.*

LOST FRIENDS

But if you don't make the effort and you don't nurture your friend or return the call or make the time to see them, then the relationship just withers on the vine. We all know how easy and comfortable it is to revisit an old school friend. You can pick up exactly where you left off. You have shared memories and shared stories, a conversational shorthand that makes everything so easy. But then the time between contact lengthens and the gap between meetings grows ever larger, until it is not months but years since you last saw each other. We are not quite sure when a friend you don't see very often becomes officially 'lost', but eventually there is a point of no return when the distance between is too great. There is too much to be said. Too much to catch up on. The shared memories are too faint to be relevant and finally the conversation becomes so stiff and hollow it is too painful to go there at all.

F *It is weird to think what they are up to now. There are some it would be so hard to meet again as you would have to go through everything. I am sure that is partly why we don't meet up – there is too much to get through. Too much to say. I have mates I see once a year where it still works but it is a rare thing. It makes me sad to think about it. Particularly if you split up for no reason. It is like meeting up with an old boyfriend you know you can't or won't see again. It is very sad indeed.*

H *I do often think about people I used to know but the gap between us has just grown too big. I did see a group of mates the other day I had not seen for ages and it felt very weird and quite uncomfortable – we just didn't have very much in common any more. They felt the same way, I know. I am sure they were desperate for me to go! It was lovely to see them but also I think we all knew that it was not going to work again.*

THE DISPLAY OF ULTIMATE FRIENDSHIP

So you've been mates for a while, years even. You've cleaned up after many a boyfriend, you've wiped away the tears, you've drunk the wine, you've been honest about the electric-pink hot pants, you've behaved, you haven't been sick on the new sofa or slagged off the wrong lover, you've made the phone calls, you've replied to the texts, you've paid for the cab and not asked for the tenner back. And you are STILL best mates. What do you get at the end of it all? A medal? A cup? A badge? A very strong cocktail?

Being asked to be a godparent or a bridesmaid is surely one of the greatest joys of being a friend. There is nothing greater, sweeter or more lovely. It is one of the great 'gifts' that one friend can give another. It is special. Very special indeed.

F *When Holly asked me to be her bridesmaid I cried my eyes out. It was really special because I had never been one and I had only ever been to one wedding in my life.* Four Weddings and a Funeral *was the best film and although I don't want a big wedding myself, at some point every girl dreams about having a huge big white wedding and to be part of Holly's was an amazing thing. When you are young and in the playground you always say to your mates, you can be my bridesmaid and you can. So I am totally thrilled to have made it on to Holly's list; it was a real honour.*

H *I remember asking Fearne so well. It was one of the happiest moments of my life. I asked her when we were all at a party and we'd had a few drinks. It was lovely. I had seven bridesmaids and they were my seven most important girls. I had two old friends, two new workmates, two siblings and my goddaughter. It is the most important gift you can give as a friend. Although Fearne did do one thing for me which was amazing. I always said that if I had a tattoo I would have three stars behind my ear, and when I asked her to be my bridesmaid, she went and put three stars behind her ear. So she has my tattoo for me, as it were. An amazingly lovely thing to do.*

night I asked Fearne
to be bridesmaid

These roles are obviously a huge honour and extremely important and not to be taken lightly.

H I turned down being a godmother. My first boyfriend – I must have been eighteen at the time – his sister had a baby and we had been together for three, three and a half years, and she asked me to be godmother and I said no. I thought the chances were that I would not be with him and I was so young I thought I couldn't say yes – I would be the ex-girlfriend turning up. 'Hi, only me.' I bet they thank me for it now, but I think she was a bit hurt at the time.

F I am godmother to one boy whose mum is a good friend of mine and who I love more than life and it is really special and amazing. When I was first asked I just said, 'Yes, yes!' But I think I underestimated what it meant. It is wonderful to have a bond with someone and watch them grow up. I really want to set a good example to my godson. His mother says that she is proud of my work on Comic Relief and Sports Relief and I never thought of it that way. That anyone would notice. So I am pleased and proud to be a godparent.

THE GODSON, BRAM, AND HIS 'GOTH MOTHER'

DOING SPORTS RELIEF

CLIMBING MOUNT KILIMANJARO
FOR COMIC RELIEF

FEARNE AND HOLLY'S LISTS

FEARNE'S LIST

5 THINGS THAT MAKE A GREAT FRIEND

1 Someone you instantly love. I have literally fallen in love with most of my best mates as soon as I met them.

2 Listening is such a big part of being a friend. Someone who can listen to you whinge and moan and go round in circles. We all need to vent.

3 Little thoughtful gestures are such a treat. One of my mates cut out a heart from the A to Z with my new house street in it and framed it. A gorgeous, thoughtful gift.

4 All my best mates make me laugh so much. Laughter is the most important part of a friendship; getting the euphoric giggles with a mate is the best thing in the world.

5 A friend must be able to forgive all your bad points. I know I can be intense, hyper, too chatty and a bit sensitive at times. Good friends will always see through your bad points to the real you!

5 WAYS TO LOOK AFTER A FRIEND

1 Random acts of kindness. I love getting my mates little gifts for no reason at all.

2 Obviously you must remember all birthdays, anniversaries, important days, otherwise you shall be banished to crappy-friend-land.

3 Always text or call back within the hour. A good mate never leaves it any longer unless something serious is going down.

4 Always hate their ex-boyfriends. You must agree with every bad thing mentioned about said ex and agree he is the worst specimen on Earth (even if you thought he was OK).

5 Be honest (in contradiction to the last rule). Sometimes you need to be honest. It's so hard when you love a mate that much but it's needed in some situations, such as if your mate is going down a bad path, struggling with something or is blind to the obvious.

5 REASONS WE LIKE EACH OTHER

1 I love Holly because she makes me laugh. After a few glasses of wine it's Laughter Central.

2 We are so similar in some ways but SO the opposite in others and I think our personalities complement each other.

3 She teaches me about being a woman without meaning to. She is so domesticated and grown-up. It is inspiring just to go to Holly's house.

4 We get each other's job and lifestyle. We can moan and rant till the cows come home and never think badly of each other for doing so.

5 She always has good solid advice to give.

our hotel room in LA, it was
like our suitcase had thrown up!

5 GREAT MEMORIES OF US TWO TOGETHER

1 Our holiday to LA was so fun. We drank cocktails by the pool all day and partied at night. Our hotel room was gross. The ultimate girlies' holiday!

2 Holly's wedding. I was a bridesmaid and was so nervous and excited. My dress was a bit big for me and my boobs kept popping out, but bar this the day was perfect! Holly looked like an angel and I cried when I first saw her on the morning of the wedding.

3 When we were filming Holly and Fearne Go Dating, we were based at Hell's Kitchen and spent our rehearsal days and filming nights sending love letters to Marco Pierre White. He was not amused but we loved it and laughed so much! Marco still hasn't responded.

4 My fifties house party was a mega fun night. We all dressed up and danced all night. My mate Lucy was really excited to meet Holly and spat drink all over her fifties frock by mistake as she laughed when she went to say hi to her. Holly was not particularly impressed but laughed afterwards too.

5 Another time when we were filming Holly and Fearne Go Dating we were driving around Hull in an open-top car (oh, the glamour) and a massive bird's feather landed in my mouth mid-sentence. We laughed hysterically non-stop for at least fifteen minutes. So silly but so funny at the time!

5 TOP MATE NIGHTS OUT

1 Nothing beats cake, tea and chatter round my kitchen table. Some of the best laughing fits have happened in this way.

2 Going out for a dance. Me and my mates recently went out to a themed night where we dressed up in wedding attire and danced to cheesy wedding hits. Such fun!

3 Bowling is one of my fave nights out. We used to go every Sunday in a big group but we've got out of the habit. I must reinstate this pastime!

4 Going out for a lovely dinner. Food and mates: two of my favourite things in the world. I would opt for sushi and cocktails.

5 Doing something different sometimes feels daunting or too much of a chore but is always brilliant fun. My mate Lolly was recently in an interactive play in an abattoir and we all dressed up in Halloween-style outfits and went to see her. Such an unusual and fun night out.

Holly's List

5 THINGS THAT MAKE A GREAT FRIEND

1 Truthfulness – it might be painful but is always the best policy.

2 Trust – once broken, always hard to get back. Same for boyfriends!

3 Understanding – we can't always be around 24/7, what with the demands of modern life, but it doesn't mean we don't care.

4 The ability to laugh in their face but also to be laughed at.

5 Listen – sometimes friendship requires you to be quiet and listen.

5 WAYS TO LOOK AFTER A FRIEND

1 Don't go to ground, at least text back! Make the effort, even if your new fella is the most adorable thing on Planet Earth!

2 The small gestures mean a lot – postcards, trinkets, cupcakes!

3 Treat them, such as giving them a pedicure while they offload life's troubles.

4 Make them a playlist of your fave songs every six months. Fearne made me a giving-birth playlist. I treasure it!

5 Tell them, let them know that you're lucky to have them in your life.

5 REASONS WE LIKE EACH OTHER

1 We understand each other. She's always up for a laugh and she's one of the most positive people I've ever met.

2 She does the best 'come to bed' dance ever . . . ask her!

3 She grabs life by the balls and isn't afraid not to conform. I admire that!

4 She makes an awesome banana loaf.

5 She is just like me but way cooler and with way more tattoos.

5 GREAT MEMORIES OF US TWO TOGETHER

1 LA, girls' hols – what happened in LA stays in LA!

2 Fearne getting a manky pigeon feather stuck to her lipgloss while driving in a drop-top car. We nearly died laughing!

3 Me, slightly too merry, trying to put up a dartboard with a power drill in my garden so we could have a tournament!

4 The night before my wedding day, watching The Slipper and The Rose.

5 Singing Mark Ronson's 'Stop Me' at the top of our voices on the way back from seeing Prince at Koko in Camden.

5 TOP MATE NIGHTS OUT

1 Karaoke . . . sounds like a bad idea until you're the last one standing. Song of choice: 'Buck Rogers' by Feeder.

2 At either end of the sofa, chatting, with your own wine bottle.

3 Summer festivals.

4 Dinner and a movie doesn't only have to be for a date.

5 Double-date. Wouldn't it be great to get that rare feeling of your best mate's fella and yours striking up a friendship?!

A large and yet hopefully proportionate slice of our cake has to be taken up by the opposite sex! Sources of pleasure, pain, fun, fury, entertainment, misery, laughs and, of course, love: men are one of the most difficult and challenging aspects of our lives. It is the age-old story of not being able to live with, or indeed without, them.

Although one of us is fully blissed up with her husband and new baby, the other is still out there fighting the good fight for all the single ladies – and neither of us has forgotten what it's like to be out there, slaving away at the coalface of the dating scene, having our hearts broken and confidence shaken. We have both survived many a year, or three, in the arid boyfriend-less desert and in those months and years we hope we've seized that opportunity to learn many fantastic and different things about ourselves – mainly the joy of girlfriends, the pleasure of a bottle of cold white wine and of our own company! On the other hand, having walked around the relationship block more times than either of us care to mention, we both have 'form', as they say, and this much we do know . . .

My first party with boys, obviously
playing it cool... not!

THE WORLD IS DIVIDED INTO SUITABLE AND UNSUITABLE MEN – SO WHY DO WE WASTE SO MUCH TIME PICKING THE BAD APPLES?

You know the score – there are six nice boys sitting in a row at the bar, each nursing a pint and a nice smile, and one Sod arrives who should have a Government Health Warning stamped on his forehead. And who do you spend the whole night trying to flirt with? The Sod, of course. Why do we do this to ourselves? Why can't we change the pattern and go for the nice guy instead?

I always used to go for bad boys or boys who looked bad. I think it's because I was really square so I wanted to live vicariously through them. I thought they could make me look like I was a bit bad even if I wasn't. I was a cool-searcher. I wanted moody cool boys who wore black so I could do all the chatting! The wretched artist who liked music, poetry and all that crap was just my type.

While there is no doubting the appeal of the Sod, the treat-them-mean-keep-them-keen cliché is a cliché because it is true. We both hope that by the time we hit our late-twenties we might have grown out of them, or at least their appeal might be waning somewhat.

You always live in hope that you are the miracle woman who can tame the bastard. But that is never true. It is a total waste of your time and energy. It is just asking for problems.

Over twenty-five, you have hopefully learnt to love yourself a bit more and not end up with boys who make you unhappy and make you feel bad about yourself. Eventually, through a bit of experience, you realise that all you want is someone nice, someone who is a good laugh, someone you want to have a family with. You realise you are too good for the bloody lot of them.

Although that's not to say we want a man who is a pushover.

Soppy with flowers is always a turn-off. What we want is someone who cares and isn't flippant.

For us the ultimate man is a bloke who is not afraid to be a bloke and a man who realises that the 21st-century girl might earn her own money, have her own career, ideas, thoughts and opinions, but that doesn't mean that occasionally she wouldn't mind being looked after. It is a fine line to tread, but is it too much to ask?

H It's not so much flowers, it's things like ordering a cab so that I don't have to. Taking the male role, the lead, having ideas and opinions, being man enough to take control.

SO HOW MANY FROGS DOES A GIRL HAVE TO KISS BEFORE SHE FINDS HER PRINCE?

Judging by our track records, the answer seems to be loads! Granted, kissing has to be one of the best things about dating.

F A snog is the best thing in the world.

You are supposed to learn over the years to leave the Frogs alone. However, that doesn't mean we haven't had some corkers along the way.

H *I nearly went out with a stripper from a gay club in Brighton! I don't know what came over me. He was straight and very nice, but all the same. We arranged to meet for a date at Victoria Station. Fortunately my mate stopped me before it went any further. But I don't seem to learn. I met a very handsome man on the plane to Miami once. I couldn't believe my luck, he was so good looking! We chatted all the way there. We swapped numbers. I was so excited. We arranged to meet when he came back to the UK. When I walked through the door I was stunned. There he was, in a full-on cowboy outfit: the Stetson, the chaps, the embroidered shirt – I thought, am I missing something? Is this fancy dress tonight? But those were his everyday clothes. As they say – I made my excuses and left.*

F *One of the worst boyfriends I ever had was this bloke who was obsessed with cleanliness and tidiness so much so that if I left the shower wet or any water on the bathroom floor, he would get really uptight. Any water on the splashback in the kitchen, or a scatter of sugar on the sideboard from my coffee – these were all MAJOR problems! All the labels needed to face the same way on his creams, pots and shower gel – it was impossible to live with him. In the end I began to panic about it all, because I was always worrying about how he would react. It made me very unhappy indeed.*

WHY IS IT THAT BLOKES NEVER ASK US OUT?

In the olden days dating was much easier. The rules of the game were practically written down on Jane Austen's dance card. Girl liked boy. Girl smiled at boy. Boy got the hint, bowed nicely and asked your father if he could take you for a stroll around the rose garden and that was it – you were engaged! Well, almost. These days, however, things are so much more complicated. You can turn up to your local watering hole in your best jeans and highest heels and dance like a nutter all night, throwing the sexiest shapes, give it all the hair flicking and pouting you like, and still go home alone! Because the boy at the bar was too scared to talk to you, or didn't even notice that you fancied him.

F I have had to ask out all the boys I have ever been out with, except one. What is wrong with them? It started with my first boyfriend. I spotted him when I was on holiday and I thought life is too short not to give it a try. I started with the girl he was with and worked my way in through her. I thought they might be dating until she mentioned he was her brother and I thought, I am in there. From that point on I thought I might as well go for it, what did I have to lose? I do think women have an in-built judge of things. We are quite intuitive about how to play situations. There was one boy I fancied in my local pub – I flirted with him the whole time and he never noticed me. So I did the five-second-rule thing where you stare into someone's eyes for five seconds – if he looks away, thinks you're a psycho or asks you if your contact lenses are stuck, then at least you know he is not into you. But if he holds your gaze, then that's really good. And he held it! So I thought, I am in. He eventually came over and asked me if I had a cigarette and we ended up chatting in the car park and having a snog! I went out with him for four months. It may not have worked out so well in the end but I think it's important to know the score. It's definitely better than hanging around waiting and not knowing. But it's always me who makes the first move.

Having said that, who wants a bloke who comes over all champagne and credit cards? The sleazeball who thinks he can buy your attention with a glass of warm Chardonnay is not the man you want to go home with. Beware the lone stalker.

H If you are with a group of girls and a group of blokes comes over and they all chat to the girls and then one singles you out, you are probably on to a winner. A man working it on his own is kind of scary.

WHO ARE THE DANGER MEN TO AVOID?

Quite apart from the Sod, there's a group of men we have learnt over the years to avoid like a very vicious and ugly plague. The first of which is possibly the hardest . . .

The Ex-boyfriend

We've both been there, done that, worn the ill-fitting T-shirt, and thought to ourselves, what is the point of going back there? This sort of situation only ever ends in tears, and usually yours. If the man has dumped you then moves on, immediately, he is never going to see the light. No amount of new outfits, haircuts or pounds lost are going to change his mind. No amount of mad drunken telephone calls are going to make him have some fantastic road-to-Damascus conversion and see how amazing you are. And if you fall back into bed with him, it will be like reopening an old wound. It will hurt like hell and take even longer to heal. And even if you did the dumping, it doesn't make it any easier. There is a saying that reheated soup never tastes as good. And it's true.

I am a great one for going back over old ground. I have been out with a couple of guys twice. I can't help but think it is like when you buy a pair of shoes you love that the shop only had in a size too small. You didn't care because you loved them so much. One day you decide you can't wear them any more because they hurt. Then six months later you see them again and you think: 'God, I love those shoes.' And you squeeze into them and they're OK the first wear and then you feel the pinch again and you remember why you stopped wearing them in the first place.

Leopards don't change their spots. There is a reason you split up in the first place. You would do well to remember that no matter how nostalgic you feel, no matter how delicious the wine or the sunset or the last dance – our one solid piece of advice is: step away from the ex!

F *Although, perhaps, I don't know . . . I have a friend who is married to someone she was split up from. These relationships should come with the warning that there is hard work ahead. But I don't think that it's impossible. I think time is crucial too. If it is a recent ex-boyfriend, it is a lot harder than one where time has been a healer and all that stuff. Should I shut up now?*

H *Yes! Ignore her. Don't go back out with an ex. It is simple as that!*

Your Sister's or Best Friend's Ex

There is probably no greater 'No, no, no, no!' than stepping out with your sister's or best mate's ex. Even if they say they are over him, they are not. Even if they say he is the biggest, most revolting snake in the grass, don't listen. You will never be forgiven. Never! One way or another, it will end with your sister, best mate, mother, brother and everyone else in your gang NOT talking to you. Ever again. It is not worth it. Don't do it. Walk on.

F *There are enough men in the world. The simple question is – why would you?*

H *I agree. It is absolutely a no-go area. Quite apart from the fact that it would just be very weird. Imagine being with someone and knowing that your sister had been there first?*

The Best Mate

They've been with you through thick and thin. They've seen you dance like a prat, cry like a baby and devoid of make-up first thing in the morning. These relationships are precious, very precious, and not to be frittered away after a bottle of Baileys, or just because you have no one else to hug on New Year's Eve. And once you've crossed that Rubicon, you can never go back.

If you do go there, you have to be really, really sure. It can either lead to marriage or never speaking to each other again. You're taking a real chance. If you think you are going to be Monica and Chandler, think again. That sort of thing only happens on TV.

You are the luckiest person in the world if that happens. There is nothing more wonderful than falling in love with your best mate, but on the other hand, don't do it if it is not going to go anywhere. Don't just snog them because you have run out of options or you are feeling a bit lonely. It is the ideal situation but let's be honest, it happens very rarely.

The Married Man

Actually, perhaps he should be at the top of our list! But unless you have very liberal parents they are normally off-radar, until you enter the workplace and then you'd be amazed how many of them come crawling out of the woodwork. Who knew there were so many blokes who, after a couple of glasses of wine, are so 'misunderstood' by their wives!

When I was single I couldn't believe how many of the men I was meeting or who were trying to chat me up actually weren't single. I was totally shocked.

They have never really gone for me. But then I only fancy the lazy young boys so I would never attract anyone who was a grown-up!

But if they do start beating their way to your door, the answer is simple.

Just stay away. It is a horrible situation. It is someone else's husband and that is not going to make anyone feel good about themselves.

ONCE A FIRST LOVE, ALWAYS A FIRST LOVE?

Everyone can remember their first love. The way their heart beat faster at the mere mention of his name, the sickness at the pit of your stomach, the way they smelt, the aftershave they wore, the way you couldn't eat for days. The endless wardrobe changes before you went to see them. The hours spent lying under a tree together looking at the sky. The days spent saying a lot but absolutely nothing on the telephone. It is the best feeling in the world! And then, of course, it ends and you feel like someone has ripped out your heart and used it as a trampoline. You lie in bed for weeks, wearing black, in mourning for your life, listening to deeply depressing music, shovelling in the cake. We have all been there, yet somehow we each think our experience is unique. Which, of course, it is.

H God, I remember it all so well, like it was yesterday. I went out with him for four years from the age of eighteen. He was very stabilising for me. He made me realise that I wanted a relationship and a family. I learnt contentedness from him. I'm sure for the right girl he's being a great guy as I speak but he wasn't the right guy for me.

F I am still friends with my first love. We met when we were fifteen and I went out with him on and off for about five years. We didn't break up so much as sort of realise we were better off as mates. I was working and he moved on. I still see him occasionally. I am very fond of him.

VIRGINITY

Now this is a tricky one. There are some people who believe that virginity is something to be treasured, something that shouldn't be given away without thought and even saved until marriage. We both believe it is something that shouldn't be given away early or lightly. You should know what you are doing, and know the consequences of your actions, and you should be in control and not hassled into a situation that makes you uncomfortable or unhappy. It should be entirely your call, and any man who ever tries to persuade you otherwise is a man you should not be with. Having said that, we would not be living in the real world if we didn't acknowledge that things sometimes don't work out according to plan!

F *I lost mine to my first love who I had been dating for quite a while before we actually felt ready to do anything about it. I was a good girl!*

H *I am not telling you how I lost mine! My mum might read it! But I think whatever you want to do at the time is the best thing for you. Just so long as you are in control of the situation.*

First Date

So having asked the 'nice' boy out – or perhaps you have even been lucky enough for him to have developed the *cojones* to ask you out – we have a few suggestions about how to make it slightly less of a disaster than some of the first dates we have both been on.

What to Wear

The trick is to pretend you always go out looking like this. That you haven't made too much of an effort.

H Don't buy an 'outfit'. You don't want to get Grazia *and then go out and buy the Look of the Week.*

Simple is best, and if you are going to wear a short skirt, then remember the tits or legs rule and don't do cleavage as well.

HOLLY

F *Don't look like you have tried. T-shirt, jeans and some nice shoes. Look like you have just popped it on. This old thing. Boys also don't like much make-up. Effortless and plain, like 'I didn't dress up for you'.*

Where to Go

The thing about first dates is they don't have to be too formal and sometimes they don't even have to be a date. There is nothing wrong with a cup of coffee, or even lunch, if you would rather not commit to the pressure of an evening.

F *It is always good to have an exit.*

H *Leave him wanting more. That's one of the hardest things to do.*

So an early evening drink is a good idea. Saying you have somewhere else to go at 9 pm gives you an exit should you need it. But it also makes you appear popular and busy.

F *Or go to a gig?*

THE BOOBS OUT/LEGS IN OR LEGS OUT/BOOBS IN RULE.

H *Then you have to dance! Or nod in time!*

F *And reveal your music tastes at the same time! OK, a gig is a bad idea. Group bowling, with mates?*

H *Oh, I am not sure about that. I hate bowling.*

A mutually appealing venue, then, is all that is required, at any time of day or, indeed, evening.

What to Drink?

'Not very much' is the answer to that question, as both of us will testify.

 I have ruined a date with drink. I was so nervous I drank for an hour before at the pub, and then I drank cocktail after cocktail, I was swaying and I couldn't speak, let alone focus on the writing on his T-shirt. I ran to the loo, puked and made a sharp exit out of the back door, not even saying goodbye to him. He really sweetly rang my mum to see if I was OK. I went out with him after that!

 I think the rule is to stay clear of white wine. If you are going to drink, have a glass of vodka and tonic or a G&T, and then have a glass of sparkling water and then have another. But don't go near white wine. It sends you mental. It makes you really keen on talking, and makes you love the sound of your own voice – which is not good on a date. I become an oracle when I am on white wine. I think I know everything, and everyone should know that I know everything. It's a girlfriend drink, when you want to talk at each other for an evening, taking it in turns!

What to Say?

It is not so much what to say, as how much to say. We don't know what's worse – a girl who never stops talking or a girl who doesn't say a word. You are supposed to listen politely to what the bloke has to say and ask interested (presuming you are) questions.

Basically don't follow my example! I had one bloke who didn't talk and I ended up with a mouth as dry as a flip-flop as I just went on and on. He made me tense up and I just rabbited and rabbited on. There was a void and I vomited right into it. Now I would just leave the silence and let them do the work. But then I just talked one long stream of what I suppose must have been absolute rubbish. Actually at the end of that date we left the restaurant together and he tripped over really badly and we both burst out laughing. That broke the ice thank God! Otherwise I don't think he would have ever called me again.

The Goodnight Kiss

To put out or not to put out? We always find this is the best bit and the worst bit of the evening, as it is so hard to work out what the other person is feeling, or thinking. Only you can truly read the situation. If in doubt, don't go for it. Because, take it from us, there is nothing worse than closing your eyes and puckering up your lips, only to open them a minute later to realise you are standing alone in the street and the bloke has buggered off.

H I am a terrible example! I have often kissed a boy out of guilt. We've gone out to dinner and rather than see his long, disappointed face I have just given him a snog to get rid of him. Which is wrong, obviously!

But let's say you've had the kiss and it worked out. He didn't mistakenly shove his tongue up your nose, or in your ear – both of which we've had – and you're on to stage two or even three. The next big question is: sex?

H If you are newly single and you want to let off steam and have a good time, and you are safe and happy about it all, then that's a choice you have to make. But if you really like this person and you want a long-term relationship, then hold out because it is better to wait a bit. The sex will be better, for a start. You want to leave it just long enough that it is not an issue, but at that fantastic point where you want to tear each other's clothes off. When you brush past that person you are going to explode there and then.

We are speaking in an ideal world, of course.

F Then again, we all make mistakes. We think we have found Mr Right or at least Mr Right for Now, we play by the rules and things still go wrong.

TECHNOLOGY N' DATING

My sister and I, She's me with brown hair!

This is not a subject your grandmother, or indeed your parents, would understand because when they were dating, lovers made arrangements they kept. They didn't let dates hang in the air. There was no possibility of blowing somebody out moments before they were due to rendezvous. Telephones were as mobile as the red boxes on the corner of the road and computers were things that only brainboxes like Stephen Hawking would use. Blackberries were a fruit. Orange was a colour. And everyone more or less knew where they stood, or at least that they were definitely having a drink Tuesday week. Now, of course, everything is fluid, mobile and much more complicated. There is a whole new etiquette to everything, but all we know is that texting is no way for a bloke to communicate with a girl.

H   When my sister first started dating Dave, her now husband, he actually rang her rather than texted her, and we all said, 'He's a good one, don't let him go.' It was really weird and we were all so impressed that he called!

F   I got dumped by text. It was one of the most unpleasant things ever. He wrote: 'I can't do this.' And that was it. No communication, nothing else. Over. And nothing for the next three months. When I caught up with him again and asked why he never responded to my text, he said, 'I thought you wanted to be left alone.' It's a lazy way of communicating. You don't know or think about how the other person is feeling. Things can so very easily get misunderstood or misinterpreted.

Although emailing someone can be kind of romantic!

F   Emailing is a really good way to get to know each other. If you ask for someone's phone number then you have kind of got to take action, but it is so much safer to hand out your email address. I had one boyfriend I just emailed for three weeks before I actually spoke to him. They got more and more flirty until he actually asked for my phone number and then he texted me and then he called me eventually and then we met after that! So we had almost a month's worth of communication without talking once – but it was the best flirting I have ever had! You can say things you would never dare say on the phone. You can joke and develop in-jokes. You can see if you have the same sense of humour. It is quite nice – like an old-fashioned romance. Like being pen pals! The art of writing is alive and well in emails. And when we did finally go on a date we ended up having a brilliant laugh because we knew each other so well.

DRINKING AND DIALLING

The man who invents a breathalyser and puts it on our mobiles will be made the Patron Saint of Girls about Town. Phones and alcohol do not mix. There is nothing worse than that clammy, sweating feeling of dread when you wake up the next morning and scroll through your phone and work out who you might have sex-pested at 1 am.

H All I ever think is, oh it's fine, it's fine, over and over again. And it is never fine – don't do it. You think you are being clever and you are not. Not at all.

F Nothing good is ever going to come of it. I have a friend who always deletes the numbers of men she thinks she might end up calling when drunk. But the problem is she's started remembering the numbers off by heart – deleting them is not enough!

The lesson is that if you have a drink-dial problem and you are liable to lose your cool at some stage during the proceedings, then leave your phone at home. If, however, you need it, then entrust it to a more sober and possibly more grown-up friend, who will stop you from calling, no matter how drunk, weepy or belligerent you get.

H And another thing. Don't ever photograph your naked body and send it to someone! The one thing that anyone has learnt from a certain footballer's mistake is don't photograph and send, or even photograph in the first place. They will hang around forever to haunt you!

Also, apps can make a man – or at least tell you rather a lot about him.

H The last thing you want to do is date someone with a Tiger app on their phone. It's the app that removes text messages from both people's phones after they have been sent. So if you are flirting with someone you shouldn't be, you can send the text and know it will disappear an hour later or whenever it is programmed to. If a bloke sends you a text using Tiger – run a mile!

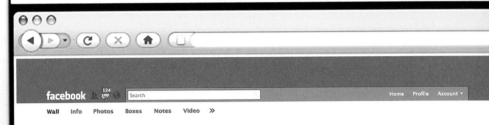

FACEBOOK AND TWITTER

The problem with new technologies and new ways of communicating is that the dangers are hidden and it's only by making a complete tit of yourself that you learn what you should and shouldn't do.

F I was on Facebook and I broke up with someone and I thought I'd better change my relationship status, and when I did this bloody great big broken heart came up on my page! It was a nightmare! It took over the whole page. I think it was weeping as well. Awful. I got all these messages – are you OK? Are you all right? It was mortifying.

As well as being embarrassing, it does also offer another modern-day dilemma: should you meet people from MySpace, Facebook or Twitter in person?

F When I was younger a guy MySpaced me. This was when it had just started about five or six years ago. He was a musician and kind of good-looking and he was from LA. And I said I was going over and for a second I thought I might meet up with him, and then I thought, what am I doing? I don't know who this guy is at all! He could be a mad man. So I cancelled the meeting.

Should you even flirt on MySpace, Facebook or Twitter?

T *I would never flirt with a stranger on Twitter. I would send a nice reply but that's about it. I don't see any point it is communicating with anyone I do not know via the Internet unless it is a harmless thank you for something. Other than that, I keep my distance. But if you are going out with someone who publicly tweets you, that's a sign he wants everyone else to know you two are dating! I have 700,000 followers so it is like shouting it from the mountain-tops – they are making sure lots of people know! You can also tweet something to show what you are doing and pretend you are having a wonderful great life to annoy them. Or you can communicate with someone else whom they did go out with to score points.*

Then if someone tweets you, do you tweet them back, or do you Facebook them? Text them? Or do something as old-fashioned as call them?

T *I had a boy who Facebooked me the other day within minutes of meeting him. It was weird – I thought it was a little keen! I also thought it was a good sign but then the problem was, do I email back? Text? Facebook? What do I do? It is a whole other thing to worry about! These things like accepting people on Facebook or following them on Twitter, they are all new modern branches of friendship. I had a boyfriend recently I didn't follow on Twitter or Facebook, and I think it was a sign that we were not really together, that we weren't trusting each other. We still wanted our secrets.*

Talking of secrets, could you, should you, spy on your current beau or ex? Or do yourself a favour and not bother?

F *It's great — you can see who they are talking to, the pictures on their site, the ex-girlfriends who are floating around. It's a great way to keep tabs on them.*

H *That's dangerous. I hacked an ex's email account once and then I sat and read all his messages and I thought, what am I doing? The only person I am hurting here is me. It is irresistible but it is no help. Knowledge is not always power.*

F *That is true. I had a boyfriend I suspected of something and I thought, if I look at that email, I am going to get the answer. And I got the answer: that he had been with someone he said he hadn't been with. It was the beginning of the end. But you know, if you think you have been cheated on and you have the access, I don't know how anyone could not.*

H *I don't want anything to do with an ex once we've split up. I never want to see them again. I never speak to them, least of all look at their bloody photograph.*

F *Oh I do. I think it is all part of the 'sitting in the rain listening to rubbish music' mourning process that you have to go through.*

And although we think this is all a bit of a laugh, that we are just whiling away a few hours fiddling around on Facebook, chatting on MySpace, firing off a couple of tweets here and there, there is a permanence to all of this that should make us question what we are doing. Who are we saying things to? And who else might be reading?

H *I think this stuff makes us very lazy in our communications and it also means your dirty laundry is up on the web for all to see. If you spend hours putting up photos of you and your boyfriend only to break up a few months later, your next boyfriend can see exactly what you've done and where you've been. You are kind of losing your mystery. On a very basic level, when we research people for* This Morning, *the first thing we do is Google them. It's amazing what you can find out. When I was looking for a nanny, I put her name into Google and her Facebook page came up. I could see everything she'd been up to.*

F *I know, it is so useful, isn't it? If you fancy someone you look them up on Facebook, 100 per cent. I have done it so many times. I have gone through friends' Facebooks to look at other people and to look at their pictures. It saves you so much time. You can see what they are like, what their hobbies are, what they look like when they are relaxing. It's instant information. It is not always the best barometer as it is slightly heightened but it does save a huge amount of time.*

Relationships

Having hopefully avoided the Sod, the best mate's ex and the married boss, we find ourselves in a happy and successful, mutually satisfying relationship. That does not, however, mean we are home and dry. Firstly the circle of two has to widen a little, and this usually includes your lovely, perfect, charming, interesting and interested friends, and his, er, 'mates'.

Meet the Mates

We have both lost count of the amount of times we've entered a dark, sweaty sitting room and, by the light of some low-rent DVD, been introduced to a gathering of mumbling boys, only for us then to perch, half-buttocked, on the arm of a sofa and feign interest in some crap film. Meeting your other half's gang of mates is a nightmare. They tend to be non-communicative and not interested in the latest girlfriend on the scene. But the main thing is not to be intimidated by this. You do not have to be the person to entertain them; you don't even need to make a first impression. Play it cool. You have plenty of time to win them over.

The thing that lets me down is my inability to stop talking. I just gabble and gabble at them. I often think if only I managed to shut up, it would save me so much embarrassment.

Equally, don't take any crap. If they are being irritating and annoying, then you are perfectly within your rights to retaliate.

I remember meeting my boyfriend's mates and they were all medics and arrogant and arsy. I had just started modelling at the time and I was like fodder for them. They took the mick all night and eventually I had had it and I went downstairs and I thought, if I am having a rubbish night, then so are you. So I smashed the fire alarm and then I left. They had to evacuate the building and wait for the fire brigade. After that they were all great. Maybe I'd earned a bit of their respect!

Their mates might, on the other hand, be the most fantastic group of entertaining men ever to gather together on one sofa. In which case, you should enjoy their company, laugh at their jokes and get every single one of them on your SIM card. The only word of caution we offer at this point is that you shouldn't abandon your own life in favour of his. You should keep your own life going, call your own mates, see your girlfriends, maintain your own relationships. Don't let his life take over yours – because if it all goes wrong and this one doesn't work out, there is nothing worse than opening the door on the way out and realising there is no one else out there.

Boyfriend + mates

Introducing Him to Your Mates

Remember, this can be as bad for him as it was/is for you. No matter how much you know and love your friends, we think that less is probably more. There is no need to parade the poor bloke around like some show pony for all to see and pass judgement on. Just as a darkened, sweaty room was threatening for you, a bright kitchen with seven girls perched around a table all drinking tea/coffee is enough to terrify the Calvins off a bloke. Boys like dark places with plenty of background noise so they don't have to talk. Think pub, think one girlfriend at a time, think no need to show him off immediately.

H There is an argument for just taking him to a big party where all your mates are and he can flit around and meet everyone and have very small snippets of conversation and then that's job done. I think it's much harder to do it one at a time, like an interview. Perhaps small groups are best but make sure you have one of those mates who smoothes things over and calms things down so that nothing tricky or untoward develops.

F It is not something you should do too soon, either, as it makes it obvious you really like them. Also, it is important at the beginning to have a selfish bit of time where you discover the good bits, the bad bits and the best bits, and then it is better to do the introducing in groups and quite sneakily. Something like, 'Hey, do you fancy lunch or a cup of coffee? And my friend Kye might come along too.' Don't make a big deal about it. Or mention, like Holly said, that your mate is having a party and they should pop in. So you can see how they react when everyone is a bit drunk and not really paying much attention. It has got to be done quite carefully as friends' approval is one of the most important things ever. Friends can really change your decisions on things. My friends are so important to me. I can't imagine life without them so it's crucial that they get on. Having said that, I have had friends who have said get rid of him, get rid of him, but it usually takes me years to do it!

Last day of school term.
L-R Polly, me, Emma, Hayley, Ruth, Ally AKA camhdio +
lucy! All with mandatory last day of school bunches!

outside Brighton icerink after my Birthday party
Clearly Black and white was
the New errr... Black!

Can You Restyle Him?

We know you are supposed to love someone for who they are, and not what they look like, but some outfits – such as the head-to-toe football kit in man-made fibre – are just impossible to get near, let alone love.

H   *Anyone you cuddle and get an electric shock off is really bad – you don't want to go there.*

So we are both of the opinion that it is not wrong to reshape and remodel your man – just so long as you are tactful and subtle as you go.

H   *If you are trying to change someone's moral fibre, then you are going to get nowhere. You can tidy things but you can't change people fundamentally. If they are not very image-conscious, you can slowly change their stuff. I have dressed a lot of men. My husband was a project but now I have given up. He's a bit of a lost cause. He'll announce, 'Today is about patterns.' And then walk in wearing dogtooth and check just because he wants to. I have changed him a bit from an Essex boy to more of a country gent – there are fewer go-faster stripes down the side of everything.*

F   *I think it is all about stealth, slowly slowly you get to restyle that monkey! I have a mate who has restyled her bloke by finding a nice shirt and buying it in bulk and then she gives them to him one at a time and he just thinks he is getting presents. Little does he know he is being totally made over!*

ME AND DAN

HOLIDAY TOGETHER

There are a few situations in a relationship that prove to be the make-or-break moment, and going on holiday together for the first time is one of them.

F *It is true that after a holiday you know if you are compatible or not.*

H *I remember being keen beforehand and then the whole thing falling apart because we went away and this guy didn't tell me anything. Nothing. No stories, he knew nothing. I found myself sitting on my own with the guidebook – it really put me off him.*

So if you are sure you're ready to go away with your new man, both of us think the trick is not to set off to Australia. Play it safe and a bit closer to home.

F *I have panicked when I've gone away and thought, oh my God, it is just him and me in this room for the weekend. So don't make it more stressful than it has to be, don't travel too far away! And make sure there is plenty to do, so you don't both end up sitting there staring at the walls. A city break is good, with lots of restaurants and art galleries. Although it has to be somewhere neither of you has been before. You definitely don't want to be walking in the footsteps of an ex-girlfriend!*

Once you've decided on your destination, then you are likely to be sent into a panic over what to pack. We have a mate who once went away and forgot to pack anything for below the waist – she had plenty of tops and no bottoms at all.

Carte Postale

𝓗 But don't turn up with all of your Agent Provocateur sexy pants in your bag as you will freak him out. Just your normal M&S undies are enough. Don't pack a huge bag – you never wear much on holiday – and get everything waxed!

However, one word of warning. When you share a room with your boyfriend, you have to be prepared to also share a bathroom. Most of the time this is OK, but sometimes it can be excruciating. It is hard to maintain your mystery when you are very unwell indeed . . .

𝓗 I had a terrible upset stomach in Kenya and just couldn't bring myself to go to the loo in the same room as my boyfriend, so I was making stuff up about getting out of bed in the middle of the night, pretending to order drinks from the bar! I kept coming back with bottle after bottle of champagne, all because I wanted to go to the loo! It was awful, a terrible experience I'll never forget.

holiday to Sardinia in 2009.

Meet the parents

This is a big step! If he wants to introduce you to his parents, then it means he plans on you sticking around for a while – unless he still lives with them, that is! So if you also plan on sticking around for a while, then good behaviour is what is called for. And rather like on the first date, less is more when it comes to meet-the-parents' clothes. The shortest skirt and the lowest top might set his dad's pulse racing, but it is not him you need to impress.

It is all about the mother. It is all about charming her. If you think you are going to come across as scary or mad, then notch it down a bit.

Don't say, 'Hi, Mum!' It is just the worst.

We both think that if you can suggest a meeting in a restaurant or café, it might make a sticky situation a little less stressful.

Don't meet at their house, take the pressure off. Have lunch or tea or something not too tricky. And try to get other members of the family there too. It makes it more informal.

However, meeting on neutral territory in the right clothes, armed with some pleasant conversation, and not calling his mum 'Mum' is not a guarantee for the perfect parents' meeting, as both of us know only too well.

I remember meeting one boyfriend's parents at a restaurant where the chef cooks in front of you. The chef said, 'Who wants to catch a prawn in their mouth?' And the mum's boyfriend says yes. And he catches one. Then the mother does the same, as does my boyfriend. I try and, of course, miss. I get hit in the face by a hot prawn and all this chilli sauce goes into my eye. It's burning, my eyes are watering, I am pretending to be OK. My mascara is running down my face; all the sauce pours down my white T-shirt. I just wanted to go home and die.

H *My husband took me back to his mum's house and introduced me to his mother, who had four kids, she's Italian and is very keen on family. He thought it would be funny to say, 'This is Holly and she doesn't believe in family.' I couldn't believe it. I thought, what the hell . . . ? It was a nightmare. I spent the next twenty minutes telling her all about how much I loved the idea of family, how families were brilliant, and it was all I ever wanted. It was the worst start ever.*

FEARNE WITH HER DAD

HOLLY'S MUM AND DAD

MOVING IN

This is perhaps the biggest step you can take beyond actually tying the knot and is not something that should be entered into lightly. You have to be very careful what you want out of this situation, and you also have to protect your money as well as yourself. Renting together is different and a lot less risky. If you are both putting the same amount of money in, then you also have the same amount to lose. But if you are buying, you should remember that your cash or capital took a long time to earn, and should not be given away. Equally you must be careful that, if the relationship breaks down, you are protected if you want to leave.

F   *You don't want to tie yourself up financially and not have a way out.*

H   *You don't want to find yourself having to stay somewhere because you can't afford to move out. I lived with someone once and we had a joint mortgage and when we broke up it was like getting divorced. It was very painful. It is always painful and always difficult. You have to be sure before you make that move. The more thought you put into it before, the better. You need to have it in writing.*

We also both think that if you are taking steps towards marriage, then living with your man before you set off down the aisle is essential.

F *You learn so much about them. When I went out with a clean and tidy obsessive, I could not have guessed what he was like if I had not spent time at his place. If I only socialised with this man, I would not have known any of that madness.*

Also, when you live with someone, you go through the process of doing up a house together – which can be good, or bad!

H *My husband and I are very similar in what we like and dislike so we enjoyed doing up our house.*

F *I like stuff, collecting things, buying things. The obsessive man came into my place and said, 'How can you live like this?' And I thought he was joking. And it was then that I began to have doubts. I like living in a cosy house and he likes living like a robot in a cold metal box – you have to have the same sensibilities or it's never going to work.*

That said, when you live with someone you also do learn the fine art of compromise. You learn that it is not going to kill you if someone puts the milk in first in your tea, that your bacon doesn't have to be dead, dead crispy and *Top Gear* on a Sunday night does, indeed, have its moments.

F *You have to open the door to let someone in. You can put up so many barriers and obstacles that in the end it's just you, your record collection and a couple of cats.*

H *I have a friend who has been living on her own for years. She lives in a place that is packed with cats and rubbish, and finally a bloke moved in last week and she sent a skipload of stuff into storage. I think she found it rather cathartic.*

So the nice boy turned out to be another Sod/Frog after all. If you dumped him then the situation should be relatively easy to handle. Guilt aside, he wasn't right for you, and fortunately you saw the light in time before you married him – well done! Reward yourself with some new shoes and a night out with the girls. Don't go back there, obviously, as it will only prolong his agony and mess with your own head. So hold your head high and keep on moving forward. If, however, he dumped you, then it is a completely different story. You might be able to get over the situation with plenty of chocolate Hob-Nobs, a girlfriend's shoulder, cups of tea and some energetic dancing to 'Independent Woman'. Either that, or you could spent the next few weeks sitting in your car in the pouring rain listening to your 'tune' over and over again, and fingers crossed you're cured. Here are a couple of things you do not want to do.

Don't become Psycho Girl

Hanging around his house, calling his mobile, turning up at his pub, badgering his friends, lying weeping in his front garden . . . However much you think this behaviour is justified, however much you think you are getting away with it – trust us – you are NOT.

The more you pretend not to care, the better it is. Stay away from alcohol and anywhere he might be. If he dumped you, don't try and get back with him, as he doesn't want you any more – end of. There is no winning him back. He dumped you. Don't ring or beg or give him abuse, otherwise he will only say, 'I am glad I got rid of her. I was right.' Move on. Find someone else. Call your best mate.

the break up hair cut

H̶   There is an expression that in order to get over a man you need to get under another. To me it seems better left in an episode of Sex and the City. *If you are feeling emotional and vulnerable and fragile, then perhaps a girls' night out is equally good medicine!*

Don't have a Break-up Haircut

You know the ones. You're walking past a hairdresser and, on a whim, you sit on the chair and say: 'Get rid of it, shave it off, dye it another colour.' It is supposed to make you feel better, to get that man right out of your hair. It doesn't.

FEARNE HAVING A BAD HAIR DAY!

F I have cut my hair off, dyed it red and pink, and I have always gone 'Crap!' afterwards. It was exciting at the time and I got a rush of adrenalin, and then you're sort of stuck with bright red hair. If you want to do something – go and buy a pair of brilliant shoes.

H I have had the same haircut since I was nine, so when I split up I get rid of all the underwear I had from that relationship – every single scrap. I think, new man, new pants. I can't bear the old ones any more.

F I agree. Buy yourself three new sets of underwear and you'll be amazed what it does for you. It sends out a totally different signal.

sad songs

In Mourning...

SINGLE LIFE - BECOME A YES MAN

The trick to being single is to enjoy it. You have had boyfriends before and you will again, so this is a moment or period of total indulgence where you don't have to think about anyone else. You don't have to include anyone else, you can do entirely what you want, when you want, and it is fantastic.

You have to become a Yes Man like Danny Wallace and say yes to everything, try everything, be adventurous. I remember going to three random parties with a girlfriend. We went to a snowboarding party, a pirate party in Camden and then on to a Jamaican rum bar, which was bizarrely called Cottons, with great mango daiquiris. It was great fun. Also one night I do vaguely remember going to a gig, then to a band's album party and then to a hotel bar and then straight to work. Very messy. But you have to say yes to everything otherwise you don't meet new people or change your life.

There is also a certain element of challenge involved in being single. You should try to test yourself, set yourself goals – even if they are small, like you have to stay at the party until 10 pm before you are allowed to go home. You have to talk to three new people, or speak to the handsome man by the crisps.

H *You have to be a bit brave. I remember once thinking, it is Friday night and I am going to take myself out on a date. So I went to dinner and saw a movie (Love Actually – of all bloody films!) and I came home at the end of that night on my own and I thought, I can do this. This is great. We are all guilty of falling into boyfriend's friendship circles, with their plans, and you forget to do things on your own or get to know yourself. It was so liberating. There is nothing more empowering than realising you can just be you.*

F *I went to see Elton John on my own because no one would go with me and I had the best time ever. I was really scared and I felt like an idiot in the queue. Everyone was in couples. But in the end I loved it. I had a couple of drinks; I focused on the music and had a great time. I don't want to do it every night but it was a good thing to know that I can do it on my own.*

Having enjoyed your own company, being single is also a time when you can sit back on the sofa with a bottle of cold wine and really enjoy the company of a close girlfriend.

H *A night in with the girls is one of life's great joys.*

F *They are great. I can't think of anything I like more.*

Also you should really remember that staying in a rubbish relationship because you are frightened of being single is not a good reason. There ARE plenty more fish in the sea and you WILL find someone who is right for you. Remember, if you are hanging around with Mr Wrong or Mr Not Really Quite Right, how on Earth are you ever going to find Mr Completely Perfect in Every Way? Far better to be by yourself, having a nice time with your mates, going out doing mad, bad and interesting things, than stuck at home eating curry on the sofa with Mr Dull and Dreary. It's just not good for you.

I have lived on my own and been single off and on for the past six years and they have been the six most interesting and exciting years of my life. You are your own boss, you can come and go as you please and you answer to no one. It's brilliant.

WHEN IT GOES RIGHT

You've managed to get through the courting process unscathed and finally you end up with the One. All that Frog-kissing has paid off and you've landed yourself Prince Charming – or at least that's what you hope. But how are you supposed to know? We are both slightly sceptical about 'the One', the love-at-first-sight idea, although we do have a friend it has happened to, but we both think it is more likely to be a slow-burner relationship that lasts the course.

dressing up at bestival

F I think there is too much pressure on the 'Prince syndrome'. That you will know as soon as he arrives. Rubbish. I think it is different for everyone.

H I totally agree. The first time I met my husband I thought he was a complete wally. He was out with friends and he arrived with one arm around my mate, and one around his mate, and he was so trolleyed. And I turned to my friend, I was sober, and I said I think we should go and it was one year later when we worked together that we finally spoke. It could not have been a more inauspicious start.

But from inauspicious starts, beautiful relationships can grow. There are no rules, there are no real yellow brick roads to follow to achieve marital nirvana. Suffice it to say that when the moment comes, you should hopefully be able to recognise it and grab it with both hands.

H We were dating for two years and they were quite magical years because both of us only worked on Saturdays so we had the rest of the week to go to gigs, stay in bed late and play around. It was an amazing, very carefree time. He proposed the night we moved into our house together. I was extremely stressed as I had done all the moving because he was at work, and I had somehow managed to fuse all the lights in the house. He told me to have a bath. It was probably a lot more romantic because we had no lights. The room was full of candles and he went down the road to the pub to pick up a bottle of wine and as he did so he picked up a dozen white roses, and when he came back, he proposed. I couldn't believe it! I was so happy. I wanted to call everyone and tell them we had got engaged. I called my sister and she said: 'I know!' I said, 'How could you know?' And they were all in the pub. Dan had asked her and a few mates to come. They were all in the pub waiting! So I got out of my bath and more or less had my engagement party in my dressing gown. I was extremely nervous about telling my mum. But Dan told me she already knew! He had gone down to see my parents the week before to ask for their permission, which was amazing of him. He told me it was the most terrifying day of this life. He asked both my parents. My dad may wear the trousers, but my mum is the braces that holds up the trousers. It was one of the happiest nights of my life!

*WEDDINGS

Unlike the complicated situation with finding the love of your
life where there are no rules and love at first sight may take a
while – there is one definite rule for weddings. Do what you
like. Don't be pressured by anyone into having a Big Day with
a Big Dress if what you really want to do is run away to Gretna
Green and have a half in the pub. It is your day, and it is a
celebration of your relationship, and it is probably the only day
in your entire life when you can get away with doing exactly as
you please. So go for it! If you want to do it underwater in the
Bahamas with a vicar in a wetsuit, then that is entirely your
prerogative.

H For my wedding my rule was that I was going to be completely
and utterly selfish, and whatever we wanted we had. So if I didn't
want to invite my second cousin, but I did want to invite my
hairdresser who has coloured my hair for fifteen years, then I would.
Anyone who had any problem with that didn't care about us as a
couple. And in the end I had the most perfect day.

F I want a Bianca Jagger wedding – a white suit, a small venue
and about ten people. I would like to get married. I think it is
important and I love a wedding. Holly is brilliant at organising and
I am not. So I would like something quick and simple and over with!
My mum got married in a big, white, flared trouser suit. I think she
still has the jacket. I might use that, actually. What a brilliant idea!
I wonder if it fits?

FEARNE'S MUM

HOLLY

04/08/07

Save the date, come
to our wedding

FEARNE AND HOLLY'S LISTS

2

FEARNE'S LIST

10 SONGS TO MOPE TO

Rachel Yamagata & Dan Wilson, 'You Take My Troubles Away'

The Cure, 'Pictures of You'

Leona Naess, 'How Sweet'

Azure Ray, 'Sleep'

Coldplay, 'Fix You' (the ultimate cryfest of a song)

Levy, 'Rotten Love' (amazing lyrics)

Morning Runner, 'Burning Benches'

Bat for Lashes, 'Travelling Woman'

Jamie T, 'Emily's Heart'

Paolo Nutini, 'Growing up Beside You'

10 SONGS TO GET OVER HIM

The Do, 'On My Shoulders'

Kelly Clarkson, 'Since You've Been Gone'

David Bowie, 'Rebel Rebel'

The Gossip, 'Standing in the Way of Control'

Elton John, 'Rocket Man' (I listen to this far too much)

Smashing Pumpkins, 'Today'

Blondie, 'One Way or Another'

Rainbow, 'Since You've Been Gone'

Martha Wainwright, 'Bloody Mother F******
Asshole' (weirdly, the most beautiful track ever
and such a man-hater of a song)

Lissie, 'When I'm Alone'

Cat = keloy

5 WAYS TO KNOW HE'S RIGHT FOR ME

I wish I had just one of these, but here goes:

1 He likes my cats.

2 He is charming to my mates.

3 He doesn't freak out when I eat peanut butter out of the jar with a spoon.

4 He smiles more than he frowns.

5 He makes me feel alive/happy/gooey/fabulous.

5 WAYS TO KNOW HE'S WRONG FOR ME

I have far too many of these!

1 He is more interested in his car than me.

2 He is intimidated by my job.

3 My mum doesn't like him.

4 He is incapable of communication.

5 He has no patience with my sometimes odd ways.

5 WAYS TO MEND A BROKEN HEART

1 Call up your best girlies, go for a cocktail or five and chew the cud for hours.

2 Get in your PJs, get your mates over and watch reruns of The Office.

3 Treat yourself to something that'll momentarily cover the cracks. Make yourself feel as fabulous as you can.

4 Get ready to move on. I am pretty good at moving on in the big wide world when I know there's no hope with a situation.

5 Avoid restaurants where couples could potentially be snogging, feeding each other, gazing into each other's eyes. Go dancing instead.

fearne took this in La and sent it to me, I think it looks like a great place to live!

10 SONGS TO GET OVER HIM

Avril Lavigne, 'So Much for My Happy Ending'

Liz Phair, 'Extraordinary'

Fleetwood Mac, 'Go Your Own Way'

Destiny's Child, 'Survivor'

Ugly Kid Joe, 'I Hate Everything about You'

Christina Aguilera, 'Fighter'

Dinah Washington, 'I Don't Hurt Anymore'

Alanis Morissette, 'You Oughta Know'

Kate Nash, 'Foundation'

Lilly Allen, 'Not Fair'

10 SONGS TO MOPE TO

Elton John, 'Guess That's Why They Call It the Blues'

Four Non Blondes, 'What's up?'

Meredith Brooks, 'Bitch'

REM, 'Everybody Hurts'

Radiohead, 'Fake Plastic Trees'

Joy Division, 'Love Will Tear Us Apart'

Celine Dion, 'All by Myself'

Ben Folds Five, 'Brick'

Elliott Smith, 'The Biggest Lie'

Cat Power, 'Good Woman'

5 WAYS TO KNOW HE'S RIGHT

1 Silences aren't awkward.

2 He'll listen to your music.

2 He wants to meet your friends.

4 Playing games such as who texted who last don't matter any more.

5 You feel so content, you think you might just burst!

on honeymoon

5 WAYS TO KNOW HE'S WRONG

1 You feel like you have to get up early to apply a full face of make-up.

2 He doesn't ever take the initiative when organising a date.

3 He'd rather hang out with a lot of people than spend time together.

4 He hides his phone.

5 He expects too much from you, be it the way you look, how often you see each other or how you behave; life should be relaxed.

5 WAYS TO MEND A BROKEN HEART

1 Have a girls' night and dance your ass off!

2 Kiss someone else.

3 Have a makeover – hair, clothes or, if you're like me, buy new undies.

4 Don't live in the past, allow yourself a short time frame for wallowing in self-pity, then draw a line under it!

5 For one night only, eat your own body weight in Haribos.

WORK THE OFFICE THE JOB

CAREER OCCUPATION CALLING

THE NINE

Gone are the days when ladies sat at home and sewed a fine seam waiting for a handsome man in tight trousers and knee-length riding boots to jump down from their white chargers, whisk them off their feet and take them away from it all. As little as three generations ago, our sisters' options were limited. No choice, no voice, no cash and with little or no education, theirs was a difficult, monotonous and often depressing existence, where many women were trapped in lives they simply could not get out of.

The country was failing to use its wealth of genius and enterprise and half the nation's talent was spent washing socks and making a chicken last the week. Since then women have thrown themselves under horses, marched the streets, burnt their bras, come out of the kitchen and tap, tap, tapped away at the glass ceiling. And we are the lucky generation who have inherited the lot.

These days life is very different for your average post-feminist girl. We are expected to earn a living. We WANT to earn a living. Actually, we want a little more than that, we want a life, a career, our own independence, we want control of our own destinies, we want families and we want to be able to opt in, opt out and shape our own futures. In short, we want it all!

Both of us have been working since we were teenagers and we take our work life very seriously. After all, our working life has shaped us, changed us and really made us who we are. It has put us in the public eye and even allowed us to be in the fantastic position to be able to write this book. Our work and careers are very important and constitute a large slice of our cake. And we hope that over the fifteen or so years we have been at it we have become not only a little bit older but also wiser and have learnt something useful from our experiences.

SCHOOL AND UNIVERSITY

Although both of us started work early and didn't go to uni, it doesn't mean we don't think uni is a good idea.

I like to know what I am doing, so school suited me just fine as I had a timetable and someone to boss me about! But my school was seriously academic and I felt I wasn't that good at it, until I went to college and I realised I wasn't so bad after all. They held up one of my essays in the class as an example of something good, which was amazing. I don't regret not going to university – I was going to study psychology – but it would not have helped me in the career I have chosen. I always wanted to open a cattery and have a small psychotherapy clinic attached to it. That was the plan! I did do an Open University course when I was between jobs. I did the first year and I have the credits for it, which you keep, so I can go back to it. I think it is good to have a safety net. Having a plan B is very important.

$$x) = \sqrt{b_x(x)} = \sqrt{\left(e^{\sigma^2} - 1\right)} \, e^{\mu + \sigma}$$

FEARNE

The white Rabbit
in 'Alice in Wonderland'
Ballet production!
knock knees!

F I did loads of auditions when I was going up for adverts and theatre shows, and I was always at drama school doing ballet. I really hated school. I just knew there was something else out there other than this boring routine. I would stare out of the window in maths dreaming of this other life. I wanted excitement and I wasn't getting it at school. I had my walkman up my sleeve the whole time, listening to music to escape. I doodled. I wrote poetry. Anything to get me out. I was good at the stuff I liked, but anything else I refused to listen to. I didn't fit in very well, either. I started doing TV at fifteen and that instantly led to ridicule. The older girls were quite intimidating. My real mates were over the moon but a lot of the others just thought I was a show-off. So I was their point of abuse at school. Fortunately they did prepare me for the adult version of that: i.e. TV critics! But I think I did miss out by not going to university, definitely. Both socially, and also in that I would love to have a degree in something. But I wouldn't be doing what I am doing today if I had given up my job then. So when I made that decision I thought, I am not going to muck around in the job area. I am going to try really hard to make this opportunity work for me. And I have just kept on going. I have never thought, oh I am safe now, I can relax. I have just kept on going. In my fantasy life I would have done drama or art at university. I would love to have learnt about the whole art scene. I could have had the most amazing three years of learning about art, which would have been great. Maybe I will do it one day. Never say never.

GETTING YOUR FIRST JOB

Getting your first foot in the employment door is a major achievement and something we don't think anyone ever forgets.

I don't think you will ever feel as good or as proud as when you were chasing and getting your first job. I remember when I got Disney Club, when I was fifteen. I thought, this is the best moment ever. I don't think I have ever had such a moment of elation and joy.

But in order to get your foot anywhere near the door, you obviously have to do a lot of hard graft.

Preparation is everything. I always research miles in advance. I always have done and I still do, because if you know what you are talking about then at least you are confident. Nothing can really faze you. Even if you don't have all the answers, you should have a few. It is usually the most boring bit of the job but it always pays off.

You should also always be flexible with your first few jobs. Perhaps the thing you most want doesn't happen right away. You might have to put in the hours, doing something you don't want to do or like, in order to move further up the ladder or that little bit closer to the prize.

I was working in a TV production company during the day and in order to pay the rent I was working in a pub in the evening so that I could be in London to be near the auditions to try and get more work. All the time I was doing something I didn't want to do, I was thinking about what I was doing it all for.

HOW IMPORTANT IS NETWORKING?

In some jobs, like being a Hollywood star plucked from obscurity, it is crucial to be in the right place at the right time. In most other careers it is sadly all about hard work and putting in the hours. People harp on about networking and expanding your contacts, getting out and meeting people, putting your face about, but it is important to be realistic about this. Going to a conference is one thing, trying to ingratiate yourself around the place is quite another. It is difficult to say exactly how many jobs are dished out or contracts negotiated late at night, propped up at the bar. In our industry there is a lot of after-work schmoozing to be done and some of our colleagues are first-class bar-flies who can flit from conversation to conversation while carefully nurturing one drink and not making a total tit of themselves. Safe to say that neither of us are very good at this. We also tend to think that if the Big Cheese Boss is having a drink, munching on a few peanuts, the last thing he needs on a Friday night is a pushy thrusting youngster shoving themselves in his face as he heads towards the bar. But then again, as we said, we are rubbish at networking. And that is not to say it won't work for you – given the right bar, the right dinner, the right conference with the right boss and the right perfectly timed joke, and you might find yourself catapulted to the top of your profession in record time. If you do – tell us how it's done!

H Some people like the networking bit and don't like the actual hard work bit. I am not very good at networking but I will do it if I have to.

F I am so bad at it. I can't hold my drink and I never know who to say what to. With my work I can make decisions all the time. It is just the rest of it I am no good at.

HOW HARD SHOULD YOU WORK?

Whether you are just starting out at work or if, like us, you have been at it for a while, we are both of the firm belief that you have one crack at it – whatever it is you want to do – and you should give it your best shot. Like most clichés, the saying 'You get out what you put in' is absolutely true, and particularly of work. As is that other age-old maxim, 'If a job is worth doing, it is worth doing well.' Obviously neither of us is deluded enough to think that everyone has a job they love or a burning desire to do something they have been nurturing since they were six. We know we are both very lucky to be doing jobs that are exciting, rewarding and which we love. But we still think that if you work hard enough you can achieve your ambitions. Nothing is ever really handed to anyone on a plate, and it is all there for the taking.

F *You have to think about what you want in life and then go for it. You have to work to your own levels, do your best for yourself and not compare yourself to other people. Concentrate on what matters and where you want to go.*

H *I think you have to take pride in what you do. Even if you are working for someone else, if you feel like you're owning it, then you do it better. I never go in and think, I can't be arsed. If I'm going to be there I will be there 100 per cent. There are days when I feel a bit crap but I would never show that. Even if you are having problems, or there are people you don't get on with, you carry on and you don't let it affect your performance.*

Messing up at work

For a start, obviously, no one is perfect and we are all entitled to make mistakes. Secondly, there is almost nothing that can't be explained away, apologised for or sorted out with some abject grovelling. There are a few golden rules that might help you, such as don't be late, don't be caught making personal calls and don't bitch about your boss on Facebook/Twitter. As well as the ever-important: don't bitch or discuss private stuff in the ladies' loos. We have lost count of how many times colleagues have been caught out sharing something indiscreet across the stalls only for the boss/office gossip/rival to be in the next-door loo listening to every word. Keep you head down, keep schtum and concentrate!

F *I mess up all the time – I just hope I learn from it. The old idea that you have to be nice to the people you meet on the way up because you will see them again on the way down is so true. Many of the researchers I met years ago are now the future of TV. So no matter what position you are in, in any job, don't think you are the be-all and end-all because you could end up back at square one in the blink of an eye. Also, if you are nice, someone might compensate for your mistake, cover for you and then it won't be so bad!*

SEX AND THE WORKPLACE

The sane and grown-up response to sex in the workplace is that on no account should you mix work and pleasure, particularly over the photocopier or in the stationery cupboard. But then again, who on Earth are we kidding? Both of us have been there, done that and got a little carried away.

H I married my producer!

F You are always told not to sleep with anyone on the crew when you are working. But I remember one show where everyone was sleeping with everyone else and I had a fling with the catering chef. Well, they were all at it! It makes work much more exciting. I think it is a load of old crap that you shouldn't sleep with people you are working with. If he's married, or can jeopardise your job, then obviously not. Otherwise, if it is light-hearted and you can send cheeky emails, then brilliant. What a laugh.

Although, obviously, a bit of discretion is important as the last thing you want is for everyone to know your business as and when it happens. A bit of privacy is crucial for your own self-respect.

H Mine was a little bit more tricky. Because Dan was my producer, he used to talk to me all the time down my earpiece. And there was another presenter and I kept on thinking, this is going to balls things up, because the other presenter might get annoyed and think I was getting more attention, so we had to be really careful. You never know how people are going to react. We kept it a secret for six months. We actually managed to do it! But it only made it all the more fun.

I ♡ this picture, we'd only been together 2 weeks - looks like we're walking towards our future

You should also take into account the reaction of others. If your relationship can be seen as tactical or advantageous to you in any way, you have to be prepared for your colleagues to react negatively.

You do have to be careful because if you are a woman and if you are an attractive woman you can be accused of doing things you are not, like sleeping your way to the top. They say you are dressing provocatively, working it, and you're not. But there are a lot of unpleasant people out there, so you should be careful.

It is also true that the older you get and the longer hours you work, the choice of where you can find your partner narrows. The more time you spend at work, the less time you spend at other places and the chances to meet and mix with other people diminish. So for some people work is the place where they are most likely to meet someone. The only thing to remember is that if/when it goes wrong, you still have to work with them. Share a room with them. Chair a meeting with them. Sit in the same canteen as them. Travel back and forth on the same bus/tube/train. Is it possible to work next to someone when they've broken your heart, or you have stamped all over theirs?

In this business it is hard to meet people. I have tried going out with lots of different people, but I do know it is not good going out with someone who does the same thing as you.

I wouldn't touch another TV presenter with a barge pole – except Phillip Schofield, of course!

OFFICE PARTIES

We have all been there, drunk as a skunk, sitting on your boss's knee telling him how much you hate X, Y and Z, and, through a haze of hiccups, how he should sack X, demote Y and make sure Z never gets another job in this town again. Or even worse. You've danced on the desks, thrown a drink at someone, cried on the dance floor till your eye make-up has run in streaks down your face and ended up lying on the floor of the loos, hugging the toilet bowl as if it were your best friend. The greatest mistake to make at the office party is to think that it is a party. It is an office get-together, and the word 'party' should not really be mentioned as it might confuse you into thinking that normal party rules and normal party behaviour apply. You should let your hair down, but not so far as to obscure all reason and decorum.

H *It depends what sort of drunk you are. If you are like me and you like the sound of your own voice when drunk and think you have the best advice and that so-and-so could do with your help and a few home truths, then you should remember that although it is fun to misbehave, it is still work. Because there really is little worse than being the tale of the night. The one everyone is talking about.*

F *Don't get drunk and photocopy your arse. But that is not to say you should be the boring old fart drinking mineral water in the corner. Then again we have all made complete tits of ourselves at office parties. We all do it and it's a laugh and it is just another good fun story at work. The idea is to make sure your boss is not around and that there is someone else behaving worse than you!*

in Lake Como for X factor – They call this work!

The trick is to have a party buddy who can warn you if you are overstepping the mark, saying a little too much rubbish, showing a little too much breast, dancing a little too flamboyantly. Eat BEFORE you go, and work out your exit strategy in advance. Say you are staying till ten and stick to it. Take your mate with you and make sure that neither of you thinks it is a good idea to take the post-room boy home. Follow these rules and you should still have a job in the morning. Equally you can ignore all these and hope and pray everyone else is as badly behaved as you!

It also helps if you know who you are talking to. I remember once standing next to Fearne at this Christmas party. I was slightly worse for festive spirit, and she turned away to talk to a friend, leaving me standing with a bloke I didn't quite recognise. So trying to be polite I asked, 'What are you doing here then?' He looked a little put out before replying, 'It's my party.' It was only the head of the channel we work for! I smiled and in a blind sweat and panic mumbled, 'Nice tie.' Not a great move.

BEING UNPOPULAR AT WORK

Sometimes it just happens, things don't work out. Perhaps you rubbed somebody up the wrong way by mistake. Perhaps the group at work are so tight-knit they can't or won't let someone else in. Or perhaps your youthful enthusiasm makes the rest of them feel cynical and jaded. Either way, sometimes you can be unpopular at work. We both have a friend who left her job to have only four people sign her leaving card. Bizarrely she was hired back by the same company a few years later. She fitted in much better the second time around and when she left they threw a big party for her. Perhaps it was only after she left that she was truly appreciated.

If someone is bullying you or picking on you or giving you grief, as long as you didn't cause it and you have acquitted yourself with dignity, then you are the winner in the end. You have to rely on your reputation or build a good one so that if you are ever picked on you have something to fall back on. I had a producer once I didn't get on with at all. He wanted everything his way. We argued, and he went and lodged an official complaint about me. He lied and said that I had said something about him. I am not sure he thought it would go very far. But it went to the top and he was forced to admit he had made it up. It was horrendous.

F I did a show once with a very disorganised crew and I felt I was being thrown out doing a live show very much on my own and unsupported. I was scared. They wouldn't help so I lost all manners and respect for them. They hated me and I hated them. But that is the only time I have done that, because with any person, in any job, you have to behave properly, otherwise you'll get a bad reputation. For example, if I interviewed Brad Pitt and caught him on a bad day, I would say to my mates that Brad Pitt was an idiot and he'd get that reputation. You always have to be careful because once you get a rep like that, it is hard to get rid of. Especially when you are starting up. You have to be humble, keep your cool, no matter what you are feeling, from day one till the end of your days.

H I always believe in killing people with kindness – that is the only way to succeed. It is very disarming.

SHOULD YOU STAY OR SHOULD YOU WALK?

It's not working out. You're miserable. You're hating your job, it's not challenging you. It is not quite what you expected. Maybe you've outgrown it. Maybe you're not being appreciated. Maybe they still think of you as the sixteen-year-old crater-face who first walked into the office and handed around all the cups of coffee and bourbon biscuits. Or maybe your eye is on the prize and you need to get off your skinny-jeaned backside and go for it. All we know is that we have both been there and we know how incredibly hard it is to walk the plank and take the plunge. But do it! And don't forget to hold your nose!

F I have never been fired. But there are moments when you have to be brave. I remember leaving kids' TV to try and make it in the adult TV world. It was like losing an arm. I was shit-scared, leaving the comfort and safety of what I knew. I left and I didn't work for about a month and I had just moved into a flat, so money was tight. But I don't regret it at all.

H I had something similar when I was leaving CBBC and trying to make it in the adult television world – it was very hard. But if it wasn't hard then it wouldn't be worth doing. It was the best decision I made.

SHOULD YOU DREAM AND ASPIRE OR JUST GET REALISTIC?

Obviously by the time you are in your early twenties there are certain young dreams and ambitions you have left by the wayside. Being an Olympic gymnast or a ballerina at the Royal Ballet are perhaps no longer on the cards if you're knocking twenty-five and can't touch your toes. However, that is not to say you should totally give up on being chess champion of Europe, playing the saxophone for David Bowie or designing a catwalk show in Paris. You can dream. It is just that the dreams should be possible, or attainable in some way.

F I am always dreaming of doing stuff, most of it totally unrealistic, but I dream, anyway. If you don't dream, you have no starting point. If you say to yourself, I'll never do this, I'll never do that, I am stuck here, then you will be. Stuck. Wherever you are. You need positive energy, then you are spurred on to do it.

Although if your head is in the clouds, then you can't see where you are going on the ground. And the ground may actually not be such a terrible a place after all.

H You should try to reach a point where you are happiest. Sometimes I think you can want for too much and then you never reach contentment. Sometimes you are striving so much you don't realise what you've got. You need to stop and sit down and realise when you have a good thing, so you don't throw it all away without noticing.

THE FAME GAME

Should you dream of being famous? Is fame a goal in itself?

Not so long ago, fame used to be this irritating by-product of talent. Actors made films, won awards and became well known. Singers made records, people bought those records and they became well known. A few stars shone brightly and became very well known. But being famous was not an ambition in itself. People did things first, they had a talent or had achieved something that set them apart, something that made them a little less ordinary. These days, however, you can become famous for being ordinary, for 'just being yourself'. You go on a reality TV show for a while, say some things, drink some drink, make a tit of yourself, get interviewed a few times, go to some nightclubs, fall out of a few nightclubs and then end up going back home. It doesn't require any particular talent, nor is it particularly lucrative and neither does it really mean anything. You sell your privacy and your private life for a few photos and a table in a restaurant you probably can't afford.

F *I get emails all the time from people wanting to be famous, which I never reply to. There are others that ask about wanting to be a presenter and I will email back with some tips. But fame is the worst bit of the job. You have paps shouting at you when you are minding your own business and wandering around on your own. You have people writing rubbish about you that you can't control. It may surprise a few people to hear me say it but it's not much fun.*

H *And at least I have some money to keep me out of trouble. I have the back-up, the people to look after me, the house in a quiet neighbourhood where no one bothers me. But if you are Big-Brother-famous it's different. You don't have anyone looking after you and no slow-burn career to fall back on. Fame as a goal in itself is useless.*

WOMEN IN THE WORKPLACE

As we said earlier, the battle has been long and hard, with some genuine casualties along the way, and we are both inheritors of a very different playing field from the one previous generations of women had. That is not to say it is entirely level, because it is not. Men still earn more than women even when they are in exactly the same jobs. And given the jobs that both of us do, on-screen female talent isn't treated the same, doesn't get paid the same and also doesn't last as long (it gets traded in for a younger, firmer model). But given how uneven the surface was to start with, we have come a hell of a long way.

H The choices are all there for us if we want them. You can be a cut-throat businesswoman or a stay-at-home housewife. Or even a bit of both. Whereas the older generation of women, because they had to fight for the choices, had a lot of actual choice taken away from them. They had to be completely dedicated. For them to give up and change course would be unheard of.

F We were the first year at school who were allowed to wear trousers. We protested long and hard against having to wear skirts, and won. So we were literally wearing the trousers. I bet some of the girls at my old school are now back wearing skirts, but because they want to rather than because they have to. Whereas we wouldn't be seen dead in them.

WORKING WITH OTHER WOMEN – DOES THE SISTERHOOD EXIST?

You can get the impression that some women are so busy tapping away at that glass ceiling, struggling so hard to get through, that they'd happily step on the heads of other women to get there. There are some women who can be extremely unpleasant to the other women coming up behind them. Perhaps it is the old adage that they had it rough, so you can too. Or maybe they feel threatened by the competition. But we know that for some women, their worst enemy can be their fellow sister just across the table.

F *I think women compare themselves more in the workplace than men do. Men don't care so much, either that or they are better at hiding it. In the workplace there are always going to be some pretty amazing people who change your life, and some bad eggs you wish you hadn't met. How you deal with the bad eggs is what makes the difference. Don't take the bait – move on.*

H *I like a big powerful woman boss. I am very happy to play second fiddle to her. I get on well with women. I am not a pushover. I am just a bit more silent at getting my own way.*

However, the best thing to remember, if you ever find yourself in a situation where the sisterhood support you were expecting doesn't materialise, is that the road is long, the hurdles are many and you will get there in the end.

H *I remember one woman getting at me because of my weight. I was wearing a harness in one scene that made my hips look massive, and then in another I wasn't wearing it, and she said loudly: 'Oh, I see what you mean! It makes you look enormous.'*

F *Oooh, she knew what she was doing!*

H *People get found out in the end. I am a great believer in what goes around comes around. No one wants to work with a nasty person. I've worked on my reputation and kind of hope that people will stick up for me in the end if I ever got into a some sort of situation.*

F *I have encountered plenty of men who are difficult and unpleasant to work with, it is not just a girl on girl thing.*

H *You can use your femininity to your advantage as well. You can keep your cards close to your chest and take a while to play them because men always underestimate you. Sometimes men can be quite stupid.*

BABIES AND WORK - CAN YOU GET THE BALANCE RIGHT?

Can we have it all? It is the age-old question and one that is almost impossible to answer. We are the generation who are supposed to have everything on a plate. We are supposed to be able to climb the ladder and at the same time keep everything else in perspective. Our careers are important but unlike the Bridget Jones girls before us, we are not going to obsess about them to the extent that we forget to have relationships and babies. But at the same time we have both seen enough of our friends, mothers and cousins struggling to know that it is hard to work full time, have a baby and keep everyone else in your life happy. Quite apart from the fact that if you are freelance no one pays for your maternity leave, and there isn't necessarily a job waiting for you when you are ready to get back to work.

H Taking time out in any business is always dangerous. There is a new influx of people who are always ready and willing to jump straight into your warm shoes in about two point four seconds. You feel, if I go, will I be able to come back? But you have to work out what is important to you. I am lucky because I don't have to work all day every day, but having said that, it was a difficult decision to make, to take time out to have a baby. Not that I regret it for a second. It just means you have to work twice as hard to keep all the balls you are juggling in the air.

F You have to work out what is right for you and get some sort of balance. You have to pick the time that's right for both you and your partner and then hope it happens or works out. Mind you, I am so insecure about everything, I sometimes wonder if I will ever have the confidence to do it!

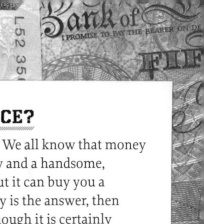

IS MONEY THE DRIVING FORCE?

At the end of the day, how important is cash? We all know that money can't buy you love, happiness, a healthy baby and a handsome, loving and loyal husband/partner/toy boy. But it can buy you a nice big fat house to put them all in. If money is the answer, then what the hell was the question? Because although it is certainly very useful and it can get you out of a tight spot, or make the spot you are in a lot more comfy with a few more cushions, it is not the be-all and end-all. Much like fame is the by-product of talent, so money should be one of the results of doing something you want to do, or something you love. If you start making career decisions solely on the basis of cash, you might end up doing things you regret, selling yourself short or compromising your once hard-fought-for ideals.

H   My whole aim is to pay the mortgage off on my house and have enough money to look after my kids and have a nice life. The fact that I really enjoy my work is a bonus. This is what makes me do what I do and not the other way around.

That doesn't mean we both agree on how important our work/money ratio is. If either of us won the lottery, would we give up work?

H   Yes.

F   No way. I base a lot of what I am about on my work. I don't know what I would be without work. I have done it since I was fifteen. I paint, but I don't know what else I would do. I have a drive, an impetus to work that I can't explain. I like getting myself into situations I have never been in before – like interviewing Paris Hilton when she asks me to hang out in her house while she dresses up and puts her fake tan on. I am terrible at relaxing. If I don't have a million things to do, then I worry.

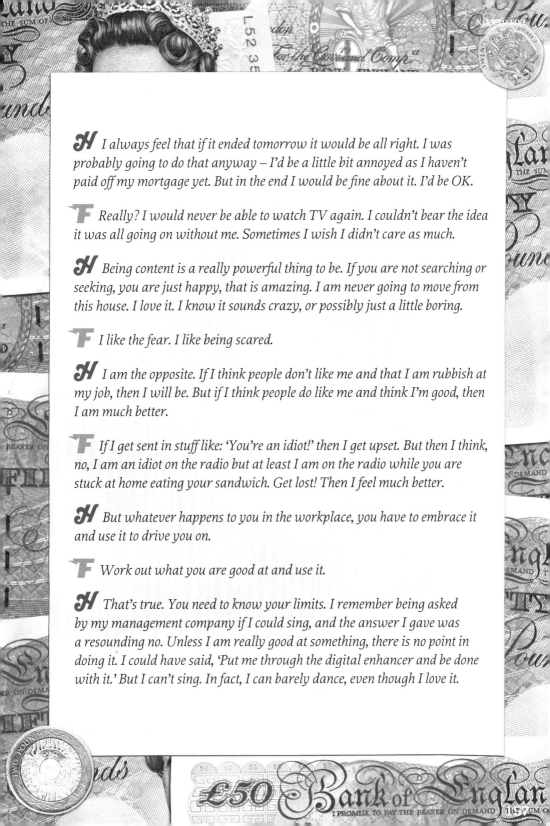

H   I always feel that if it ended tomorrow it would be all right. I was probably going to do that anyway – I'd be a little bit annoyed as I haven't paid off my mortgage yet. But in the end I would be fine about it. I'd be OK.

F   Really? I would never be able to watch TV again. I couldn't bear the idea it was all going on without me. Sometimes I wish I didn't care as much.

H   Being content is a really powerful thing to be. If you are not searching or seeking, you are just happy, that is amazing. I am never going to move from this house. I love it. I know it sounds crazy, or possibly just a little boring.

F   I like the fear. I like being scared.

H   I am the opposite. If I think people don't like me and that I am rubbish at my job, then I will be. But if I think people do like me and think I'm good, then I am much better.

F   If I get sent in stuff like: 'You're an idiot!' then I get upset. But then I think, no, I am an idiot on the radio but at least I am on the radio while you are stuck at home eating your sandwich. Get lost! Then I feel much better.

H   But whatever happens to you in the workplace, you have to embrace it and use it to drive you on.

F   Work out what you are good at and use it.

H   That's true. You need to know your limits. I remember being asked by my management company if I could sing, and the answer I gave was a resounding no. Unless I am really good at something, there is no point in doing it. I could have said, 'Put me through the digital enhancer and be done with it.' But I can't sing. In fact, I can barely dance, even though I love it.

MONEY, MONEY, MONEY – TO SPEND IT OR SAVE IT

The temptation to spend cash is everywhere. The latest dress? The latest pair of shoes? The latest iPad, iPhone, iGadget? It is hard not to lust after everything all the time, especially when conspicuous consumption is being shoved down your throat by every WAG or wannabe in every mag or newspaper you open. But if the bank crisis has taught any of us anything, it is perhaps the idea that you should not spend more than you earn.

I got the sense of money from a young age. I helped my parents buy their second house. I was sixteen, I was earning money and I was living in the house so it was right that I paid some money – not much, but a bit. I didn't grow up with money but I knew exactly what we could and couldn't have. There were lean times when we went on camping holidays – they were brilliant – but I knew the value of stuff. As a result I am very careful with my money. I am not a tight wad, but I love a bargain. I would prefer to save than spend my money on material things. I'd rather invest in my future than buy a pair of Christian Louboutins. The only things I am carefree about are holidays. I would happily never go to a designer shop ever again.

Quite apart from the fact that waiting for something or saving for it does actually make the buying of it a whole lot sweeter, credit cards are dangerous. They may well be flexible friends but they are also fair-weather friends, who get you to spend more and then disappear when the going gets tough. Credit-card debt is a nightmare. We have lots of mates who have fallen foul of the old swipe-now, pay-twice-as-much-later routine and it's not worth it. And it mounts up and up and up. We have friends who have to borrow more money to pay their bills – the circle is vicious.

F *I didn't let myself have a credit card until my mid-twenties. And I only really use it when I am going on holiday or buying something really expensive. I have a direct debit so it has to come out every month so I have no choice. I would really hate to get into debt.*

It's important not to let a bit of money or a bit of success turn your head. Don't let your first pay cheque turn you into Puff Daddy! After you've got the bling and the babes there is still the rent to pay, the food to buy, and then you've still got to get to work!

F *I could very easily have gone mental when I was nineteen and been in Chanel every day. I have seen pop stars who have been famous for five seconds going bonkers the way they spend money, larging it up, drinking champagne, buying stupid cars, and now they are in a mess. I would never let myself get into that situation.*

H *I remember I was saving for a house and I had a friend and all he wanted was a car. He couldn't afford the car so he got it on finance and then all he wanted was a Burberry umbrella so he could put it on the parcel shelf and people would think he was really cool. He spent all his money on that rubbish and he ended up with nothing.*

HOW IMPORTANT IS AMBITION?

The driving force that gets you out of bed in the morning, the thing that makes you suck up all the bad experiences because you have your eyes on the main prize or a secret burning that keeps you awake at night – ambition is a powerful thing and harnessed in the right way, it can be extremely useful.

F I am definitely ambitious. I get a massive kick out of it. I am incredibly lucky to do what I genuinely love. I have lots of friends who hate their jobs, so I appreciate it is very hard to give 100 per cent when you don't want to be there. But you still have to give it all you've got to get the result you want.

H Although I love staying at home and doing the homemaking stuff, I also love my job. My goal is to stay where I am, doing what I am doing. There is no big dream thing to hit any more.

HOW IMPORTANT IS CONFIDENCE?

A little bit of confidence can go a long way. It is amazing how believing in yourself when all around are doubting you serves you well in the workplace – and even if you don't feel that confident, if you are enthusiastic when everyone else is a little jaded then you should go far!

H None of my mates can believe I have this job because when I was at school I was so unconfident I used to talk through the sleeves of my jumper. I used to pull them down over my hands and then talk through my hands. But I believe you can learn to be confident. No one likes to be out there for all to see, but you have to be brave. And then you get a little bit braver and you get better and better at it. It is about believing in yourself – and a lot of practice!

F *I think it is crucial to believe in yourself because no one else is going to do it for you. If I believed all the negative stuff people said to me – that I wouldn't amount to anything, that I should stop dreaming – then I would never have got anywhere. Weirdly, my old English teacher, who always used to tell me never to stop thinking I could do something, is now a bestselling author – Conn Iggulden, of* The Dangerous Book for Boys. *He never gave up hope, did he?*

LOVING IT, MAKING THE MOST OF IT AND GETTING AS FAR AS YOU CAN!

So you have behaved at the office party and kept your pants on! You have worked your way up, been nice and not a diva. You are in the job you like and hopefully might be able to love; you find it fulfilling, interesting, stimulating. You are earning more than a living and the secret is to enjoy it. Work hard, enjoy the peaks and troughs, ride the wave and realise that it is not where you're going but how you get there that counts.

I think I have been doing this for so long that I don't know who I am without work. It has become me. I almost think I wouldn't be me if I didn't have it. I love it. I am especially keen on my new clothing range at the moment. I got some samples through the other day and they made me really overexcited. I can't believe someone let me design a dress, let alone actually make it up!

There is nowhere else I would rather be at the moment. It is hard work, but I like hard work. The work I do is exciting. I am presenting and designing my own clothing range. Sometimes it goes wrong, but that's all part of the journey.

I left school at sixteen and sometimes I wake up still thinking I have to go there. I hated it so much. But then it slowly dawns on me. I don't have to go! I can do what I want! Maybe that's why I don't take it for granted. And why I love what I do. I thank my lucky stars for every minute!

IN THE LIVE LOUNGE WITH ROBBIE

WITH JO WHILEY AND REGGIE

this morning

mum comes to work

FEARNE
AND
HOLLY'S
LISTS

3

FEARNE'S LIST

5 BEST CAREER HIGHS/THINGS I AM MOST PROUD OF

1 Getting my first job on Disney Club. After years of auditioning for stuff it started to feel like it was paying off. A high I'm not sure I'll ever reach again but one I'll try to match.

2 Interviewing Prince William and Prince Harry. It was a total honour and pleasure. I knew I had to nail it, as it was their first TV interview without their father present and they had to cover some painful and untouched ground. Cynics out there wanted me to fail because I am a young blonde presenter with no journalistic background, but it turned out to be an honest, relaxed, open interview, which I'm more than proud of.

3 Climbing Mount Kilimanjaro. I have never pushed myself so hard, mentally or physically. On reaching the top, I was elated – literally on top of the world!

4 Visiting Africa several times for Comic Relief. Meeting people from all walks of life, sharing laughter, tears and stories with people from such a different world to my own, is a total honour. It's one of my favourite things I get to do in my job.

5 My own clothing line. Something I've dreamt of doing since I was in the womb. When I got the first pair of shoes made with my name in the insole, I stared at them for hours!

Last Disney's Diggit show age 19.

So obviously out of my depth/scared/screaming inside etc...

CLIMBING MOUNT KILIMANJARO
FOR COMIC RELIEF

THE KILI LADIES: MAKE-UP, ELEGANCE AND GENERAL HYGIENE OUT OF THE WINDOW FOR 8 WHOLE DAYS!

5 THINGS YOU SHOULD NEVER DO AT WORK

1 Never be an arsehole. I've come across many of these over my thirteen-year career and it's never necessary and these people never last.

2 Don't throw your toys out of the pram. Deal with things rationally and calmly. I was DJ'ing the other day and one of the other performers shouted at me because she thought I was playing her backing CD from my decks, and then she shouted at some poor sound technician. NOT needed, rude and obviously driven by some kind of insecurity!

3 Don't bring personal problems to the workplace. So hard at times but no one trying to get on with things at work needs to hear about your shambles of a love life, lack of sex or alcohol problem. Leave this stuff for mates and soldier on. Believe me, I'm saying this out of experience.

4 Try to avoid making enemies. You don't want to have to start dreading work because there's someone there you have issues with. There's always one person at work who annoys you. Just try and deal with it in the best way you can and get on with it.

5 Don't nick people's food at work. You might see some tasty hummous or new cheese in the fridge and you think no one will notice. DON'T DO IT!

5 THINGS YOU SHOULD DO TO GET AHEAD — TIPS FOR THE TOP

1 Think outside the box. Use initiative and stand out from the crowd with ideas and example.

2 Stand up for yourself. When women put their foot down in the workplace it can be seen as diva-ish. NONSENSE! If done in the right way you'll get what you want and make your point without people thinking you're a bitch. Never be scared to stand up for what you believe in.

3 Work hard. If you put the work in, put in the hours, and believe in yourself, there's no reason why you won't get where you want to be.

4 Don't listen to haters. I was told for years when growing up I wouldn't be able to be an actress, a presenter or work in TV. You have to believe in yourself and have deaf ears to non-believers.

5 DREAM! I'm the biggest dreamer in the world. Some people think I'm unrealistic but I think you can do anything you want if you put your mind to it.

5 THINGS NOT TO DO AT THE XMAS PARTY

1 Don't snog a married man. This could never surely end well. Not tried this one and won't be doing so in a hurry . . .

2 Don't get so drunk you can't walk. You don't want to be known as Pisshead Paula at work for the rest of your days.

3 Don't decide this is the time to demonstrate your up-till-now-unknown party trick, i.e., look, I can do the splits while doing a shot of sambuca. Instant respect loss.

4 Don't hog the karaoke all night. I remember a work do where it was like a showcase for one individual. Not that I wanted to have a go. I would have just preferred some variation in performers that evening.

5 Don't tell your boss he's a wanker. If you are particularly passionate about this, at least leave it until you decide resignation is the only way out and then unleash your true thoughts.

1 TERRIBLE MISTAKE!!!

Singing on Fame Academy. I was pressured into doing this by people who knew it would probably be hilarious to see me trembling with nerves and singing out of key. It raised lots of money so I'm happy about that, but no one should have to hear me sing.

3 THINGS I WOULD LOVE TO DO

1 Keep my clothing line running as best I can. It's something I want to put maximum effort into.

2 More visits to Africa for Comic Relief as this is something I would feel slightly bereft without, I'm passionate about it.

3 I would also love to interview Jimmy Page!

Holly's List

5 BEST CAREER HIGHS/THINGS I AM MOST PROUD OF

1 Winning the BAFTA for Best Children's Presenter.

2 Seeing someone walking down the street wearing one of my designs.

3 Juggling work and motherhood.

4 Being asked to be ambassador of the Children's Hospice Association.

5 Having someone as respected within the TV industry as Phillip Schofield choose me to sit beside him every morning.

5 THINGS YOU SHOULD NEVER DO AT WORK

1 Lateness in my eyes is so rude.

2 Sitting on Facebook all day is a very bad idea.

3 Only start an office romance if you think it's got legs.

4 Don't use your sexuality to get ahead.

5 Don't put up with being leched at or picked on!

5 THINGS YOU SHOULD DO TO GET AHEAD — TIPS FOR THE TOP

1 Be decisive, don't faff about.

2 Work hard and keep out of office politics.

3 If you do become involved in office politics, kill people with kindness.

4 Be nice to people: it sounds simple but it does help.

5 Don't be afraid to ask for help and ask questions. Everyone has to start somewhere.

5 THINGS NOT TO DO AT THE XMAS PARTY

1 Step away from the photocopier – give it a wide berth.

2 Don't snog your boss.

3 Don't puke in the printer.

4 Don't tell everyone you love them.

5 Don't go home with the work-experience boy because you feel sorry for him.

Saturday Moring TV

1 TERRIBLE MISTAKE!

I haven't taken enough photos of my life, and I have the worst memory.

1 THING I WOULD LOVE TO DO

Show Harry the world and let him learn through life experience.

extra long
sleeves

fake
tr...

queen of heart
pockets

high u...
bl...

knot
in one
side

fake fur coat

spirograph dress.

ol hat !

chunky knit
cardi

top of
strap tied
in knot.

Back of dress

blue fabric
buttons
down
back.

ed
stretched
inny chords.

to pinch
waist dress

(perhaps cloud
print or
cream flowers or
white or light
blue). ?

black lace
heart cutout

back of
dress

© Fearne Cotton

Crush pad

Penthouse

Digs

Dwelling

Where the heart is

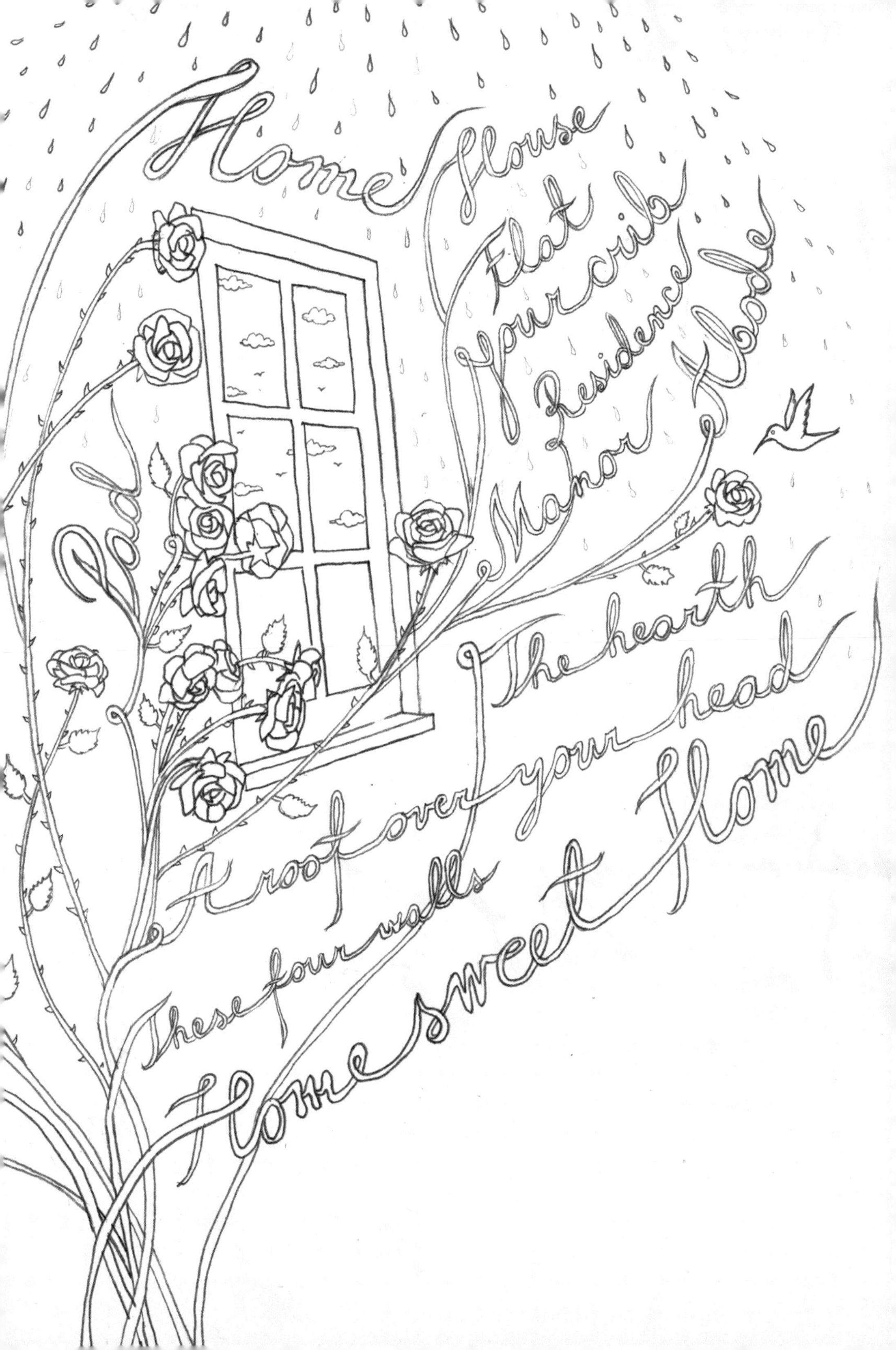
Home
House
Flat
Your crib
Residence
Manor
Abode
Pad
The hearth
A roof over your head
These four walls
Home sweet Home

We've slept on sofas, futons, sitting-room floors, shared double beds, single beds and box rooms with friends and family in places all over town. We have even, a couple of times, when particularly drunk, slept in the bath! Over the years we have both managed to claw our way on to the property ladder and after buying and selling, scrimping and saving, we each now have a place to call our own.

It has not been easy. In fact, it has taken more than few starter flats and houses, more than a few terrible decor choices and more than a few furniture disasters before we have both managed to find a home. Not together, obviously. But not that far away from each other should either of us need a bowl of sugar, a cup of tea or a large glass of very

Your place, flat or crash pad is the single most important and expensive financial decision of your life. And not only is it your sanctuary from the outside world, a place where you can totally be yourself, put your feet up, crack open the chocolate biscuits and enjoy back-to-back episodes of *Glee*, but it is also a place where you entertain your mates, have your folks over for dinner and maybe even one day have a family.

F *I have just moved into my house. It is my fourth place but my first proper home. All the other places I have had parties in, but this feels like I could have a family here if I wanted to. I have lovely friends who come around and leave nice energy. The older you get, the more your home becomes your sanctuary. I would go mental nowadays if I came home to a crazy party house the whole time. It is nice and calm here and full of my favourite things. It is so important for me to have photos of all my mates here. And all the artwork I love, and the things I have collected over the years on my travels. It is the place where all the good stuff happens. If I have had a crap day at work, then I come here and relax, feel better and think everything's going to be fine.*

H *Dan and I have been here for a while but we have only just done the place up how we want it. I love this house. I love where it is. It makes me happy. I can shut myself away here and spend hours pottering about, plumping cushions, looking after Harry. I am not moving for the world!*

F *I have only recently got the home thing. Reg (best mate and fellow Radio 1 DJ) is obsessed with interior design and he recently bought a chopping board and we discussed it for about half an hour, I think! I have never had that inclination before. I think with some people it just clicks at a certain point; with others it never does. I have mates who rent and go travelling for months to years at a time and that is their perfect sanctuary. Being a bit of a nomad, or having a place where you can house your family and keep your bits and pieces in – either is fine. Whatever makes you happy. I have cousins who are slogging their guts out trying to get on to the property ladder and it is too stressful to even contemplate.*

WHEN SHOULD YOU LEAVE HOME?

We were both rather early in flying the nest. As neither of us continued at school or went to uni, we were keen to get cracking and not hang around at home, annoying our mums, watching daytime TV and raiding the fridge. So we were out the door almost as soon as it was legal! These days, however, things are a bit different. Not only is it harder to get so much as a toe on that elusive property ladder, but also, and you should take it from us, it can be quite cold out there. Not that we're suggesting you should hang around at home till you're drawing your pension, but you shouldn't underestimate the joy of clean sheets, a home-cooked meal and someone else washing your socks!

F *I bought my first flat at nineteen. I had been saving up ever since I was fifteen to move out of home. My main goal was to save enough to get a deposit for a flat. I bought a flat in the suburbs where I was brought up. I bought it off a mate who was moving out to start a family. I was as skint as can be and I bought stuff from junk shops, made things and got the rest from Ikea. I was very serious about being grown-up. I made a meditation water fountain for good feng shui! I had a water feature!! It was hilarious. I had*

all these points to prove in the first year of living in my flat. I had my mum and dad over for dinner. I cooked, which I am useless at, but I did it anyway. Everything was spotless. I wouldn't let anyone do anything for me. I wanted to do everything myself. It was sweet, really.

H I first rented in Brighton. I must have been seventeen. I was going out with this guy. I moved into his halls of residence but it didn't work out and I thought, I can't move back home, so I rented. Most people are off to uni at that age and I didn't do that, but equally I didn't want to live at home. It was the most exciting thing ever. Not having to ask to use the phone, being able to stay on it for hours. Back then I was paranoid about money. I kept notes on everything I was spending because if you mess up at this stage, you do so massively.

MOVING FURTHER AWAY FROM HOME?
OFF TO THE BIG SMOKE?

The lure of the big city is strong. It is where the action is, often where the jobs are, and it is something both of us found totally irresistible. We both moved to town quite quickly but it was a big move, and not taken lightly. In fact, Fearne made a few moves before the big one.

F I grew up near Pinner in boring suburbia and I wanted to get out desperately. But I was terrified about moving into town at first and I was a bit overwhelmed by the whole thing. I thought if I moved into the city I might just go a bit mad so I moved round the corner from my parents. It was a good way to be responsible but in a safe environment – if I needed help, I could call Mum and she would be round really quickly.

Having cut her domestic teeth around the corner, she was ready to make the big jump and launch herself on an unsuspecting city.

F Now I have moved into town I am really excited about it and the nice thing is that going home to see my parents is like popping to the country for the weekend. And it is quite nice to get out, breathe some fresh air and get the grass back beneath my feet.

LIVING WITH FRIENDS

Forget all those nice shiny happy images of *Friends* you've seen on the TV – sharing a flat is NEVER as glamorous, or indeed as clean. At least in the early days. If you manage to get through the first year of flat-sharing without giving yourself food poisoning, getting a visit from environmental health, setting fire to the place or being chucked out by your landlord and losing your deposit, then you are doing well. For the learning curve is steep. Not only do you have to look after yourself for the first time, budget for your food and fun, but you also have to learn to live with other people, who are often less house-trained than you are.

H   I remember moving into my flat in London and that was the first time I was living with flatmates. We didn't label the fruit exactly, but I couldn't believe how messy they all were. I mean, I was certainly the tidiest, which is really saying something in those days. There was one girl who was chronically messy and who would leave everything everywhere, which was extremely annoying. But we did have a right laugh. My dad helped me to move in and we got the sofa wedged in the front door. He said it wouldn't go through. But I insisted he left it. He drove back to Brighton and us three girls all slept on the sitting-room floor with the sofa wedged in the door to stop people coming into the flat. We sat there with a bottle of white wine – it was actually brilliant. And the next day we took the windows out – with a knife, as we had no tools. We popped them out and got the sofa in that way. Somewhere in South London there is a house with no putty in the front windows! We got the sofa out the same way too.

Nutrition, of course, goes out the window too. What do you care about eating well when there is fun to be had?

H *I used to live on vodka and cranberry as one of my five-a-day and then bowls and bowls of Angel Delight.*

F *But you don't care then. You'd rather buy a bottle of Mateus Rosé and drink that than actually eat anything. I remember having terrible parties in my first flat, where we would fill the bath with alcohol and have a right laugh. When I moved out I found jellied sweets down the back of the sofa and All Sorts shoved in the cracks in the floor.*

H *I worked in a pub and so did the whole of my flat and as soon as the pub closed at 11 pm we'd say, everyone back to ours! People we didn't even know. It was fine. You let them in. I do remember trying to get the party started, spinning around on the floor pretending to be a Dalek to the Dr Who music. When the track finished everyone just stared at me.*

LIVING TOGETHER

You know how it happens. You find a nice young bloke you like quite a lot and his toothbrush finds its way into your place, or yours ends up in his mug, and before you know it you are discussing moving in together, or sharing a flat, or even buying somewhere. But moving in with Mr Right is a very big decision. Firstly, he may turn out not to be Mr Right or even Mr A Tiny Bit Right, and not only will you end up with your heart broken, but also nowhere to live. So it is important to know, if you are investing in a property and a relationship, quite how much you are putting in, and how much you hope to get out of it afterwards. We both have mates who have ended up losing their hard-earned cash at the end of a relationship, or even worse lived with someone for seven years only to find themselves out on the street with nothing to show for it, back exactly where they started.

H *I am a jump-in-with-both-feet-girl. I like living with boyfriends and I have done it a few times. I even bought a house with a bloke before. I was very careful in that I laid down the rules before we moved in together, which was a good thing because when we broke up that was one less argument to have.*

F *If you rely on someone else and think you'll just move into your boyfriend's, well, we all like to think it will all turn out all right, but you just don't know, and if you sit there and get comfortable and haven't put any money in yourself, you'll probably end up being in a bit of trouble, to be honest. You must pay something, towards the rent, towards the mortgage, so you can end up having a more amicable split if it doesn't work out. A mate of mine moved in with her boyfriend, had a baby and is now living back with her mum. Not ideal. A lot of people rush into things and this is not something to be taken lightly.*

However, that is not to say that if boot is on the other foot the situation can't work!

F *I have had boyfriends live with me. It has always been quite easy to kick them out after I have broken up with them! If anything, move in with mates until you are really, really sure. But if you can own your own property it is a real investment for the future. You don't need a man then. A lot of girls stay with their boyfriends for financial reasons. But if you can get yourself into the sort of financial position where you don't need a bloke, then that it is bloody brilliant!*

Living on your own

There is something to be said for coming home and finding no one has eaten your yoghurt, used all your shampoo and that magazine is exactly where you left it. More and more of us are living on our own and it is mostly out of choice. It is not that we have become mad old intolerant spinsters who live on pulses, stroke our cats for company and have 500 pillows on our beds; we'd like to be married or living with some handsome hunk with good conversation and a mean line in Italian cuisine. But while we look for him, or wait for him to turn up in the office, we shall have a right old laugh playing house on our own.

F   I am more than happy living on my own. I know Holly doesn't like it. If she doesn't have a boyfriend, she will always get her sister to live with her or a mate. But I have lived on my own now for about eight years. If you can do it, it is really lovely. You are in control of how you want your place to be. You can come and go exactly as you please, you don't have to answer to anyone. It is very liberating and financially it makes sense.

BALANCING YOUR BOOKS:
MAKING IT ALL ADD UP

If you are renting a place or trying to buy somewhere, you have to be on top of your money. You have to know what you can afford, what you can't and what you can save up for. You also have to know how far you can stretch yourself and how much of a sacrifice you are prepared to make.

F *I think I am more scared about paying my mortgage now, whereas before I would just think, whatever, and get the money together to pay it. The more informed you are, the more you realise how hard it is to make money and also how precarious your situation is. By all means travel, see the world and spend your money on frivolous stuff, but if you really do want a house you have to stop buying new shoes and put some money aside for the deposit.*

H *Dan and I have had to knuckle down and get the work done on the house. I suppose it is a question of priorities. If you want something, something else has to give. You can't have everything all the time and if you do then you end up appreciating nothing.*

So you have to be organised. You have to think ahead, do your accounts properly and, if you can't do that yourself, then you have to find people you trust to do it for you.

H *My mother helps to look after my finances. She has a really good money ethic. She understands the value of everything and takes nothing for granted. She chops and changes my accounts. She is of the generation that if she can save 50p, she will. She knows how much money I earn. She knows everything. She has access to everything. She has power of attorney. She has saved me so much money in the past, it makes sense. She was an air hostess and an au pair and a bit of a glamour puss, but she is far better than I am at anything like that!*

F Holly, cut those apron strings! My mother used to help me sort through my finances out until about five years ago. We lived very much on a budget when we were younger. She was always brilliant and she always made everything look good. But she really taught me how to make good with what you have got – you don't always have to have the most expensive stuff to look great. It is what you do with it that matters. Money doesn't buy you style. When I was fifteen I didn't have a clue what I was doing; she helped me set up my accounts and all that sort of thing. She doesn't any more, though. Now she complains that I don't need her any more, which of course I do, but just in a different way.

H I think if you don't have your mum to help you out you really should get someone to explain your money to you, in a language you understand. Speak to your parents. Even if you don't want them to know all about your finances, you should ask their advice as they have been running a house and paying taxes for years. It might make you want to fall asleep but you should concentrate!

ARE ALL GODDESSES DOMESTIC?

You have the house, or flat, you've got some mates to share it or you are on your own and supporting yourself, and you get bitten by the domestic bug. You take an interest in tables. Chairs are no longer things just to sit on, but they are fashion statements in their own right. Rugs actually come in different shapes. Lights don't just go on and off and prevent a corner from being dark. And perhaps your mattress should come up off the floor? How, or why, or when, this happens will depend on your nesting needs, financial means and/or your inner domesticity.

F *When a boyfriend moves in, I find myself getting a little more homely.*

H *You start buying things like a cheese grater.*

F *And a wine rack and Febreze.*

H *And that's when you stop going to Ikea.*

F *Although I am still going there.*

H *OK, you save up for a coffee table rather than—*

F *Putting some material over a couple of boxes! I must get to the beyond-Ikea stage. I just can't be arsed. And things seem to look OK. I am rubbish at this, aren't I?*

So is the moment you prefer going to Habitat instead of clothes shopping the moment you grow up?

H *That is the moment you grow up.*

F *The moment you think 'Nice candlestick!' is the moment you grow up.*

H *Or the moment when it is raining and you're walking along and you don't think, oh no! it's raining, you think, oh good the garden will get watered.*

F *That's true! When sofas are more appealing than shoes, you finally know you have gone over to the other side!*

ALL BACK TO MINE!

In the beginning there was the house party. Where sixty people you didn't know, and didn't know you, heard something was 'going down' at your place. They all decided to turn up at around the same sort of time with a rainbow assortment of alcohol, none of which went together. The alcohol got dumped into a sink, or bath of ice, and the guests tried to help themselves to something better, more expensive and colder than the drink they'd just plonked in the ice.

The party began. The music got louder. The floorboards shook. Three people were sick. Six people snogged. And the next morning you were left with a very sore head, nine black bin bags of empties and very sticky carpet.

A few years later almost exactly the same thing happens, except this time fewer people turn up and they all bring wine of various colours, vintages and quaffability. This time they don't shake the floor with their dancing, they sit on it and drink and talk and talk and drink. Three people are sick and six people snog and one glass of red wine is spilt on the carpet.

Fast forward another few years and then even fewer people turn up, they are mostly in couples or there's an even number of boys and girls. This time they sit around a table with their wine and they expect to be fed. You are expected to be able to feed them. No one is sick. Six people snog when they get to their own homes. And your carpet is nice and fluffy and smells of shake 'n' vac.

Your transition from party animal to domestic goddess is complete!

H *A dinner now is my main social event. But all I do are big bowls of spag bol or lasagne or a Sunday roast. I like big meals that people can dive into. I am not so good at lots of delicate things poised on plates for people to pick at.*

F *I am rubbish at all that. I am still in the foetal stages of domestic goddessness. I can make a cupcake and that is it. I know things could be nicer and better and tastier – I just can't be arsed! I panic when my mum comes round for lunch. I just can't do anything about it. I am getting there but I still feel I am living life like a student and I shouldn't be. I read the recipes; I am just not that good at following through with the instructions!*

H *There is a point on the road to being a wannabe domestic goddess where you just decide you want to do things a bit better and do things properly. So I decided I needed nicer stuff around me. I didn't want chipped plates. I wanted a bit more. I work really hard and I wanted a nicer environment. I didn't want to eat rubbish food so I decided to make an effort.*

Me + bezzie kye at my
hase party at New Year.

HOME IS WHERE THE DOG/CAT/RABBIT/ GUINEA PIG/FISH IS

Both of us are very keen on our pets. We're crazy about them. We both have cats. Fearne has Tallulah – named after the character in *Bugsy Malone* – and Keloy, and Holly has a very special ball of fluff called Roxy, who is so high-maintenance, his paws are not allowed to touch the floor outside. And they are an extremely important part of our lives.

H *I think pets really make a home. They make you feel happy. The house is never empty. There is always someone to talk to. You know when you get back from the airport and there is someone there? Having a pet is like having that every day. It is totally amazing and I love it.*

F *When I got my house with a garden the first thing I wanted to do was prove to my parents that I was a responsible adult, so I got two cats. But the first year was a nightmare. I was so worried about them. I had to get people in to look after them when I was away working. It was a huge responsibility that I suppose I hadn't really thought through. Now I am a bit more organised so it is easier, but there is nothing better. I love them more than anything.*

Peaches, my 1st Kitten

Cat = keloy

Mum + Wilf the dog.

The world divides into cat people and dog people. It is black and white and there is NOTHING in between. And both of us are very definitely cat girls.

H   I wouldn't get a dog, not yet anyhow. They are more work than children!

F   I agree! My mother comes over for a cup of tea and then says, 'I've got to go because of Wilf.' What? Can't you give me another half an hour? I say. But apparently not! Wilf needs her. She must go!

H   People also use them as an excuse not to do things. Like children, they are a great excuse not to go out, to come home early. They can stop you doing no end of stuff, if you need them to!

F   I am dying to have kids just for that reason – rather than saying I can't be arsed to come out. Sadly, I am not married, I don't have kids and cats are not really a good enough excuse. But the great thing about cats is that they love you unconditionally. Dogs are a little more problematic. And, obviously, being on TV I feel the need for random love from strangers. I am a need freak. So to get it from an animal is a bonus for me. I have my own private audience. Better than a man, that's for sure!

H   And they sleep with her every night!

roxy my cat

THE PITTER PATTER OF TINY FEET?

To be or not to be – a mum? That is a fairly enormous question. Birth rates are changing; the average age of a first-time mother has gone up from twenty-six to twenty-nine in the last twenty years. Women's lives are changing. We have many more choices and many more options and the ideal of a husband and two point four children is not the only show in town. Obviously one of us is a mother and the other isn't, yet. So we know what life is like from both sides of the duvet. And we both feel different pressures about the choices we've made. And while Holly's little boy is obviously the most lovely chap to have ever walked the planet, Fearne is just not at that stage yet!

F *The pressure is on for me to settle down. But I am still a few steps away from it. There are lots of things I want to do before I settle down. I want to travel. See South America. There is so much I want to see. I want to get a few more selfish bits of my life done and then I will be really ready for it.*

H *It goes in waves, I think. Loads of my mates were engaged but I was the first to get pregnant. Now I have had Harry, and they are all pregnant. But I am twenty-eight, so I am not that young to have a baby. It's just that if you live in the capital, people tend to do things a bit later. But I am not that unusual.*

F *All my work friends are having babies. But fortunately the mates I grew up with are still stuck in year 10 of school! No one has made that big step yet.*

H *I have always wanted to have a family. It is what I have always wanted since I was at school. I wanted the whole package, to be a wife and mother. I also wanted it that way round. If you want something else that's fine. If you want the baby first then that is OK. But I wanted the aisle moment in the big white dress and then the baby, in that order.*

10 days before Harry arrived

But it is a big old step and not something you can decide is not quite for you when you are already halfway through it. Babies can't be taken back to the shops and exchanged for something a little less exhausting, expensive and time-consuming.

H The one thing that has scared me a bit is that it is such a permanent thing. You can't give them back. That's what makes it all so daunting. I had the first six weeks planned and then I had no idea what I was going to do after that. It was like I had him on loan for six weeks and then I had no idea what to do. I shall have to take the rest as it comes. All I can say is that Harry has added to my life in every way. People always said you'll not believe the love you feel for your child. And I can confirm that it's mind-blowing.

F Seeing my cousin do it has made it a lot it easier. She made it the most magical thing ever and she is two years younger than me; she has made the whole thing so much more exciting and less scary. She has changed into a woman and is this amazing mum. She is wonderful and is no longer shy.

Motherhood obviously puts tremendous pressure and strain on ALL your relationships, but most especially with your husband/ partner. The mood swings, the irrational crying, the ever- expanding waist, hips, bum, legs, ankles, wrists, plus the urgent and deep desire for pineapple crisps at 3 am – these are enough to make even the closest and most secure of couples a little bit snappy. And that's BEFORE the birth. Then you've got the sleep deprivation, the piles of washing, the piles of nappies and the piles. It is much easier to do it if you are on solid ground rather than anywhere rocky.

F There is nothing worse than the band-aid-baby syndrome or having a baby for the sake of it, rather than viewing it as an extension of a beautiful relationship. They are not handbags. Or something to be hankered after or acquired.

H The one good thing about pregnancy is that it takes so long that nature slows you right down so you can get your head around what you are supposed to be doing, and what is happening. Also that visual tool of the increasing size helps the bloke, who can see it growing inside you, he can see what's happening. Life does change big time when you have a baby. But it is worth it. It just makes everything so much more complete.

F It is the natural progression from doing the partying, having the fun, getting the home together, becoming a homebody, and now you want the nice little family. It makes it all make sense. It makes it all worthwhile. I also think for anyone who has a mate who has had a baby, it changes the dynamic of the friendship. I remember going around to Holly's house after she had Harry and seeing her with this tiny baby and I was thinking, how is she allowed to have a baby in her house! I was in awe of the fact that she knew what she was doing. Someone who a week before didn't have a baby was now a mum! Here was someone I had necked sambuca with and danced with until the early hours of the morning, now looking after another human. It was amazing. But, of course, obviously you can't see each other so often, obviously she can't go out and get totally plastered, but you see another side to that friend, which is an amazing side. You do obviously feel you are losing them a bit because it is such a amazing thing that you can't really understand until you have done it. So I can't talk to her about the pains of labour or dirty nappies. I can't share that with her and it does make you feel a little left out sometimes. Emotionally you have not been through what they have been through. But I suspect that when I have kids there will be a whole new branch of our friendship that will blossom.

FEARNE AND HOLLY'S LISTS

FEARNE'S LIST

5 HOME STYLE TIPS

1 Flea markets and second-hand shops are the best for little knick-knacks that you can mix in with newly bought stuff to give your house a vintage feel. I love a good bargain.

2 My dad can print photos on to canvases at his work so I take full advantage of this by getting loads of lovely memories enlarged for my walls. I fill my house with photos to make me smile every day.

3 Recycle what you can. I have had old dresses made into pillow covers and sarongs used as throws.

4 I love things that mismatch; I like the eclectic feel of different colours and patterns.

5 Put books out on display. This sounds obvious perhaps or trivial but it's a huge part of my house. I love it when people come over and can browse the bookshelves or flick through big picture books on the coffee table. Borrowing and sharing books is one of my favourite things to do.

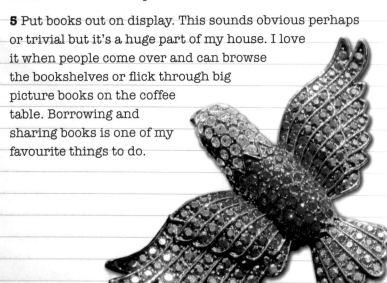

5 WORST THINGS FLATMATES HAVE DONE

I'm too much of a control freak in the house to share my private time with a stranger or even a mate. The exception to this rule is my brother, who I let live with me for three months and in this short time he managed to clock up quite a list:

1 Cereal in the sink and stuck down the plughole. This makes my blood boil.

2 Nando's boxes of half-eaten chicken left all over the kitchen worktops.

3 When he moved out he left five odd socks, six dirty mugs and four Zoo magazines under the bed!

4 I also had some American friends come over and stay for Christmas and one of them shaved his beard off with MY razor and left all the beard hair in the sink! THEN he asked me if I liked his new clean-shaven look!

5 One boyfriend who stayed over once thought it would be hilarious to blow up several condoms into giant balloons while I was at work. That day my cleaner came, tidied around them and left the balloons in the hallway!

5 RECIPES FOR THE PERFECT DINNER

1 I'm not the best cook, but I try. I go for easy options I know well. I can knock up a great couscous with slow-roast balsamic tomatoes and onions. I know this is not really cooking and more just pouring hot water into a bowl, but it tastes pretty good.

2 I'm all about the cakes. I love making cupcakes covered in camp decorations. This never fails to go down well.

3 At New Year I made a gorgeous key lime pie, which got demolished.

ME AND BROTHER JAMIE
AKA 'BROMAN'

4 I also experimented recently with blueberry crumble muffins! DELISH!

5 If in doubt, order a takeaway! Can't go wrong.

5 BEST COCKTAILS FOR A HOUSE PARTY

1 I love a simple G&T but if I'm having a party I'll mix something up.

2 At Christmas, mulled wine with tons of cinnamon sticks, cloves and oranges.

3 In the summer, Pimms with plenty of apple, strawberries and cucumber.

4 Or a punch mix with juices, fresh fruit and rum.

5 A nice simple summer drink is elderflower, gin and lemon. This is the true start of summer!

TOP 10 PARTY TRACKS

David Bowie, 'Let's Dance'

Dolly Parton, '9 to 5' (it's a reflex to dance to this)

Kings of Leon, 'Red Morning Light'

Sub Focus, 'Could This Be Real'

Britney Spears, 'I'm a Slave 4 U'

Daft Punk, 'Aerodynamic'

Michael Jackson, 'Billie Jean'

MGMT, 'Electric Feel'

Pendulum, 'Slam'

Journey, 'Don't Stop Believin'' (for the slow dance at the end of the night, singing drunkenly into a wine bottle for a mic)

5 WAYS TO BE SMART WITH MONEY

1 There are so many little things, like collecting vouchers and changing bank accounts and utility suppliers, that you can do to save money – they don't seem like much but amount to loads of savings.

2 Make your own lunch for work. I used to spend a fortune buying brekkie and lunch every day at work but now I make my own, healthier lunches, which are so much cheaper. I can then buy more shoes!

3 Buying vintage and second-hand clothes from charity

shops is an amazing way of buying unique one-offs, looking good and saving money!

4 Backpacking or camping holidays are the best and cheap as chips. I love camping so much. Me and a big group of pals went camping in Cornwall and had the best week of cooking beans on toasts and drinking cider in the rain!

5 Think of clothing in potential pound-per-wear terms. If you love something that happens to be out of your budget, you'll need to make sure you wear it a lot. Spontaneous buys usually end in tears!

5 WAYS TO TELL IF YOU HAVE BECOME A DOMESTIC GODDESS

1 I'm not sure – I'm definitely not there yet! I think when I learn to cook properly and can safely have a dinner party without help I'll get my official womanhood badge.

2 When your flat or house starts to look less like a student's halls of residence. I'm not sure I'm there yet with this one either!

3 Looking after plants. I have two plants and one of them has been on the brink of death for three years. When this plant eventually flowers again, I will be a true woman.

4 Getting excited about a light blue coffee-bean grinder to match my light blue bread bin. I knew change was a-coming when this happened.

5 When I mastered cupcakes without having to constantly look at my Nigella Lawson book, I felt such a sense of pride and overexcitement. A truly sad benchmark of becoming a grown woman!

Holly's List

5 HOME STYLE TIPS

1 Your home should reflect you, not the inside of the Laura Ashley catalogue.

2 Artwork is really important to express your own personal sense of style. I have a wall of photographs dedicated to my family past and present. It's a real talking point in my home.

3 A home is to look lived in and loved. Lots of texture and stuff everywhere adds to that.

4 Spend money on key pieces you'll have forever. Your home is a work in progress which can take a lifetime to finish.

5 Don't collect crap. If you haven't worn it, used it or eaten it for one year then it's time to say goodbye, life laundering is good for the soul.

5 WORST THINGS FLATMATES HAVE DONE

1 Refused to buy toilet roll as she didn't want someone to see her walking down the street.

2 Put dirty plates under her bed when she'd finished eating.

3 Never rinsed the bath out after using it – it looked like she'd shaved a dog in there.

4 Been very vocal in the bedroom department.

5 Used the emergency key in the electricity meter and didn't replace it, so it went off at 6 pm and we spent the whole evening and night in the dark.

5 RECIPES FOR THE PERFECT DINNER

1 Beef and chicken fondue.

2 Roast chicken.

3 Shepherd's pie.

4 Spaghetti Bolognese.

5 Chicken wrapped in Parma ham with a Boursin filling.

5 BEST COCKTAILS FOR A HOUSE PARTY

1 Twinkle: champs, elderflower cordial, vodka.

2 Champs and rose cordial – had this at my wedding.

3 Snowball: advocaat, lime and lemonade or Babycham.

4 Vodka and cream soda – don't know if it has a name but I love it.

5 Sailor Jerry's and Coke – it's a real Brighton (where I was bought up) drink.

TOP 10 PARTY TRACKS

Justice vs Simian, 'We Are Your Friends'

The Killers, 'Mr Brightside'

Candi Staton, 'You Got the Love'

Starship, 'Nothing's Gonna Stop Us Now'

Dee-lite, 'Groove is in the Heart'

Girls Aloud, 'Biology'

Strike, 'U Sure Do'

Joan Jett and the Blackhearts, 'I Love Rock 'n' Roll'

Libertines, 'Can't Stand Me Now'

Oasis, 'Cigarettes & Alcohol'

5 WAYS TO BE SMART WITH MONEY

1 Pay with cash whenever you can. Then you know what you're spending.

2 Shop around online, comparing prices using a search engine. If you then buy online, check whether the website has voucher codes; they are easy to find if you look in a search engine.

3 Buy cheap, buy twice. This is so true. Think quality rather than quantity.

4 Have a clothes-swap party. Take all the stuff you don't wear any more and over a few bottles of wine trade with all your friends.

5 Don't be afraid to make things, like cards or jewellery.

5 WAYS TO TELL IF YOU HAVE BECOME A DOMESTIC GODDESS

1 Your boyfriend/husband/partner tells you your roast is better than his mum's.

2 Your underwear draw is organised and your knickers folded.

3 You always have something to drink in the fridge – because you never know where the next celebration is coming from.

4 You light scented candles. It's really important to give your home ambiance and make it welcoming. If you are extra posh, light a candle in the bathroom.

5 You plump up the cushions on your sofa. My husband and friends will laugh when they read this. I am obsessed with my scatter cushions looking plumped!

6 And here is a bonus sixth one that is as important as the previous five: it doesn't cost a penny to make your bed in the morning. Isn't it lovely to get into a well-made bed at the end of a busy day?

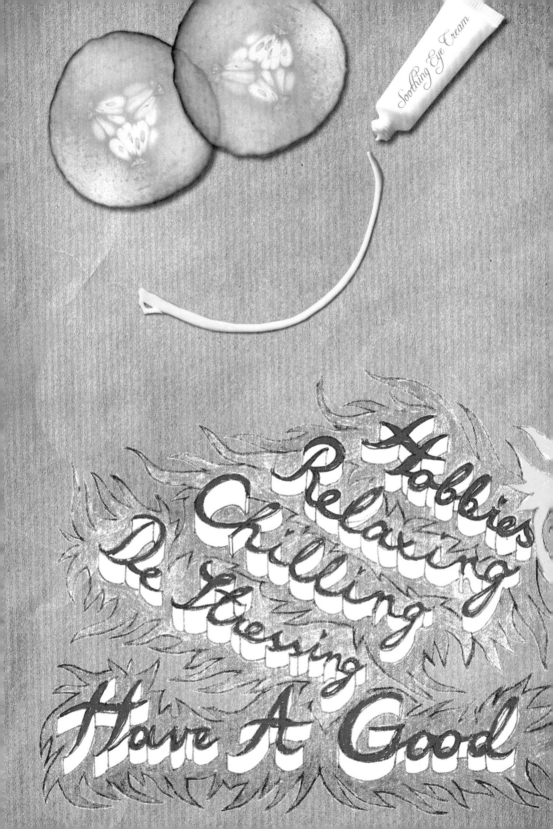

The Inner You

You Time

Me Time

Taking Time Out

Health

Beauty

Grace

Looking After Yourself

Lie Down

When all is said and done, you've got the bloke, the job, the pad and the pals, you should take a step back and a good look at yourself. You time, or me time, is important in this fast-moving world where we are expected to be all things to all people all the time. When everyone wants, expects, demands an answer to every question right now. So it is crucial to take a step back occasionally.

Pluck your head out of the water and come up for air. Otherwise you lose perspective, your sense of humour and yourself. So me time isn't a selfish waste of time. It is important time. And in order for you to keep your head while all around are losing theirs, it should be another well-proportioned, balanced slice of our delicious and this time rather tantric cake.

WHERE DO YOU START?

H Time with your family is everything. It is what life is all about. I try to spend as much time with mine as possible. Although recently things have changed a bit now that I have my own family and my other family. It was very odd this Christmas when we left to go home on Christmas Eve. My mum, dad and me, we were all crying. I was going to wake up on Christmas Day for the first time with my baby and my husband. It actually was wonderful, having my son and my husband with me. Christmas morning was truly one of life's great moments.

F I agree, family is so important. And it is interesting how these things change. Years ago I couldn't think of anything more dull than sitting down to dinner with my parents. I wanted to get out and go out. But now I can't think of anything I like more. I have also started to hang out with my younger brother as a mate, which is great. He's cool and fun and we have a shorthand which makes stuff so easy. My mother and I still manage to go back to the old days sometimes when I am a sulky teenager and she is being bossy. Some things are just meant to be!

So we both agree that family is where it's at. It's the place where we both most like to be, where we can switch off and totally be ourselves.

H Although I have just discovered my local pub. I went there for a pub quiz the other night and I have never had so much fun. I was so excited to be out that I turned into the village idiot, grinning from ear to ear.

F Luckily one of my best mates lives around the corner from me and now that I am single he is getting me to go out a bit. I felt like a teenager again dancing away the other night. I dressed up in a wedding dress and we went clubbing. I looked just like Dolly Parton. Quite weird that the first time I wear a wedding dress is to go clubbing, but anyway we had a right old laugh.

Although we agree on most things, we have a slightly different opinion on how to really kick back.

F *I have hobbies I love. I love painting more than anything in the world. I have no concept of time when I am doing it. It all goes out of the window. Sometimes I think it is important to sit down and do nothing. But I can't – the guilt I feel from doing nothing. I just can't do it.*

H *But I think you can get good at it. I think relaxing takes practice. You are forced to do it when you are pregnant and eventually you get quite good at it. It is very hard to blank out the chatter in your head but it is very good for you to try. You have to practise. At least once a week I take a moment to try and be quiet.*

F *I can't be quiet. I very rarely let myself get bored. I get bored of situations or how I look, but not actively bored. There are always millions of things I think I should be doing. There are always things I should be Googling, things I should be painting, stuff I should be drawing. I'd go mental if I was sitting on a train without my iPod. If I am walking for twenty minutes to go to the shop and back and I have my music, I am happy as a pig in shit, but if it has run out of batteries or I have forgotten it, I kill myself walking down the road because my brain is on overload and I can't stop it. It is the same when I go to sleep; I have to stop myself thinking.*

H *If you left Fearne in a room on her own for an hour not being able to do anything she would go completely mad.*

F *Whereas you would plump the cushions!*

H *That's true. I obsessively clean if I have nothing else to do. Left to my own devices, I'd go and tidy a cupboard or clean it out.*

TAKE A RELAXING HOLIDAY

If you plan to stay sane in this life, then a holiday is not a frivolous, overindulgent week away; it is an essential. There is nothing better than checking out for a week with the girls for some sun, sea and a large sticky cocktail, with an umbrella and a few virulent pink cherries on top. Where better to solve the problems of the world than lounging

- Me at Nan T.C's again Could this photo be any more 80's?.

FEARNE

by a pool, soaking up some rays and chatting about nothing in particular with your eyes closed? It's good for the soul. It makes life worth living again. It takes you out of yourself, takes you away from all your worries and reminds you of the simple pleasures in life – like swimming at sunset, laughing till your ribs ache and sleeping past 7 am! Although sadly since we have more commitments than we used to, like babies and regular jobs, it is that little bit harder to find the time to get away from it all.

H I just love going away. No sooner have I finished one holiday than I am ready to book another and that is my new plan in life. I always have something to look forward to, something to aim for. I think it is really important. Especially in the winter months. My job means I have the holidays of a school teacher and I really want to make them count.

F I've got no holidays planned at all. But I am in total work mode at the moment. I am completely obsessed.

US in LA by the pool drinking a Mojito at about 10:30am.

H You will go mental.

F What do you mean 'will'? I am mental.

H Fearne needs a holiday right now. Before she burns out totally.

F But I am in total work mode.

H But that is no use to anyone if you are stressed and exhausted. You'll only get ill.

THE FUNNEST TWO WEEKS IN LA - DRINKING DAIQUIRIS DANCING AND SLEEPING IN LATE

Flirting with boys in LA

LOOKING AFTER YOURSELF: HOW MUCH BEAUTY IS GOOD FOR YOU?

So if we are a bit different when it comes to time out and trying to switch off, and relaxing and nursing our inner chakras, when it comes to looking after ourselves with lotions and potions and unctions – we are at TOTALLY opposite ends of the spectrum! One of us is high-maintenance, right up there in the clouds being pampered and pummelled by the spa gods along with the rest of planet showbiz's finest. And the other is low, really . . . fabulously low!

H   I do, I admit, have the potential to be a bit of a slut. I know everyone says you should always take your make-up off before you go to bed, but if I didn't have those make-up wipes things I wouldn't bother. I keep them beside my bed and I just about manage to lean over in bed and wipe my eyes. They are my saving grace. But I am lazy. I have been known to go to bed with full make-up, including stick-on falsie eyelashes, and to wake up the next day, look at myself in the mirror and think, that doesn't look too bad. I'll keep it on for today as well – with the same old eyelashes, the whole thing. I think, bargain – two days for the price of one. Perfect.

HOLLY

F *Whereas I am a product-obsessed, wash, tone, cleanse and moisturise princess. No matter how paralytic I am, I always take everything off and cream my body. I get into bed like a slithery seal. I cream my whole body, each of my tattoos, everything. I will often take all my make-up off as soon as I come off camera. I don't like the feel of it on my face. I also think it is worth making the effort to look good now, so that I can keep my face looking better for longer.*

H *You sound like an advert! I can't think of anything more disgusting than going to bed covered in cream. Moisturising every tattoo? If I can take a short cut, I will. I am big fan of dry shampoo. It's great if your roots are coming through as it gets rid of them a little bit.*

F *Oh I agree with that. Mark Hill has just got one out which is amazing. His stuff is great. I have had my hair dyed every colour of the rainbow – blonde, black, red, back to blonde, ginger, bright white – and it was a frizzy, dried-up disaster, then this guy Mark said: 'Right, I am sorting this out.' So now I put leave-in conditioner in my hair at night and let it all soak in and then wash it out in the morning.*

H *Oh my god! You see? I mean, who the hell has got time for that? Only Fearne Cotton. The rest of us can't even be bothered to get our hair cut. I never use any of the products I have. I get given loads and I am afraid to say I give most of it away. The stocking fillers my family end up with at Christmas are amazing.*

F *Whereas I use everything. But I am not THAT high-maintenance. I don't do things like manicures or pedicures. I do my feet once a year and I do my hands myself as they are always in such bad condition. But then I am obsessed with things like nail varnish. I am like a teenager. I have every colour and every shade, every sparkle. I have about twenty or thirty shades. I put them in little drawers.*

But then again there are other ways to treat and pamper yourself. There is nothing more brilliant than lying down, being up to your neck in bubbles for hours and hours and hours!

H *If I have a day to myself there will definitely be a bath in there somewhere. It is my perfect relaxation state and I have had a TV put in there. I have the*

biggest bath in the world, light lots of candles and put something great on the TV and I just sit there and relax. I am always filling up the bath when it gets cold. I have to have all my limbs hanging out of it when they shrivel up and then I put them back in.

F *Oh god, I totally disagree. I hate baths. I have one every couple of weeks and I think, I am going to really enjoy this. I start to read and then I think, why am I not in bed doing this? Why am I in water? And then I get straight out again.*

H *You're mad. When I am on holiday I will have a bath every day. Everyone else can be on the beach or by the pool and I will be in there, in the bath, for about an hour. It is one of my things. I love it. All the smelly oils, the bubbles and all that stuff.*

F *I don't mind the lying down but I'd rather be massaged. I could be massaged all day. I have a very bad shoulder and as soon as I get stressed, I get anxiety issues and the shoulder always gets it. And reflexology, I think, is black magic. I love a foot massage. I'd do washing up for a week if someone gave me a massage. It is better than sex any day.*

Looking after yourself is obviously important. Making the best of what you've got is smart. If you don't respect yourself then no one else is going to do it for you. Not that we are great proponents of the increasingly vacuous 'you're worth it' culture but we think that maybe a leaf out of both our books is probably the way forward when it comes to you time. Perhaps moisturising all your bits and leaving conditioner in your hair overnight is a little excessive, but then trying to keep your eyelashes on for nearly a week is not so wise either. So don't feel guilty about taking some time out to look after yourself. Equally there is nothing so dull as a girl who takes hours to leave the house, or who can't be spontaneous, or who won't go out because she needs to wash her hair. Our advice is *carpe diem*, and invest in some wet wipes, dry shampoo and maybe have a long hot bath more than twice a month.

TV IN THE BATH.

HOW IMPORTANT ARE DIET AND EXERCISE?

This is a subject both of us feel quite strongly about. Working in television and being in the public eye, the pressure to be a size zero is huge. There are so many magazines around that berate us for being too fat and then weeks later write that we are too thin, that we've become Lollipop Girls with big heads and tiny bodies – when the irony is that nothing much has changed. These are the same mags that seem to delight in bad bum bikini shots or papped snaps of celebs falling out of cars, falling out of their dresses or out of a club. Fearne has made a documentary about eating disorders and was horrified to discover an old photograph of herself being used on a pro-anorexic website. We are very conscious about how many unattainable, airbrushed, doctored images women get bombarded with. But both of us know it's not about being thin, it is about being healthy. Life is not about denying yourself things, but about having a little bit of what you fancy. Everything, as they say, in moderation.

-Sport Relief cycle . The Ninja on a bike ! Geek!

F *I work out four or five times a week. I really enjoy it. I am a bit of an exercise nut. I love being healthy.*

H *I do nothing at all. Absolutely nothing!*

F *You worked out for your wedding.*

H *Did I? Oh yeah, I joined the gym. But I only went about eight times. I thought when I got pregnant I'd join a gym to go and swim. But I only went twice. It is £68 month, so it has cost me about £300 each time I have gone. I could have gone on holiday for that. I find it really boring. I can't bear it. I would much rather go for a big walk. But I do have to watch what I eat. I have to stop myself from really going for it otherwise I would be huge. When I was pregnant I was careful otherwise I would have stuffed myself and eaten every chocolate bar in sight. But normally I have a little bit of something I fancy. But I have to be careful. I am normally a size twelve – and that's it. My weight stays the same; it doesn't fluctuate that much. But I was a late developer. I didn't get my hips and boobs until I was seventeen and then they went bang and bang – and I was very much a woman.*

F *I am still waiting for that to happen!*

There's one thing that gets our goat more than celebs who pretend they don't diet or exercise to maintain their tight butts, and that's the celeb who boasts about her weight loss, or snapping back into shape twenty minutes after she's given birth.

H *It drives me mad when people in the public eye lose weight and then they get written about like it was some huge achievement. It's not. If you want to do it, do it for yourself. Don't tell everyone about it!*

F *I agree. Attach a celebrity to a diet and suddenly it becomes cool and everyone wants to do it. Kids who are vulnerable with their food grab hold of anything like that and that's why I always try and put out a very positive message about food. I am a vegetarian, I eat well, I don't deny myself things. I eat chocolate and all that. AND I exercise properly. I have been the same weight since I was fourteen. But I have to make an effort to stay that way.*

To nip & Tuck or not To

Your nose is too big? Your boobs are too small? You have a muffin top? Thunder thighs? Your smile is grey? Your lips are lean? Your backside is not quite as peach-perfect as you would desire? Plastic surgery is no longer just for the rich, famous and infamous – there are salons and clinics all over the country offering to lift, tweak and separate you into a more fantastic, plastic version of yourself. So the question is, do you embrace your faults? Or do you succumb to peer pressure and go under the knife? It is hard to resist when all around are pumping up their lips and chests with collagen and silicone, filling their cheeks with Sculptra, freezing their lines with Botox, sucking their fat, lifting their faces, tattooing their eyebrows and lasering their nasal hair. Where do you start? Where do you draw the line? And how do you stop ending up like the Bride of Wildenstein?

F I think the answer is to be yourself and not do anything. You should learn to love your faults and lumps and bumps. By all means exercise but I wouldn't do anything else. I am addicted to tattoos but I would never have work. I absolutely wouldn't. I would not mess with my face at all.

H I wouldn't do anything now, at all. But when I am older I absolutely would. I have no doubt that I will have Botox and fillers and my boobs put back. I guarantee. I will.

F Really? Oh no, thanks. I don't think you should touch anything. My nan has the sort of face I want. There is a story there. She looks fabulous. I want to grow old gracefully. I don't want to get all shiny and tight and miserable-looking. And they all look the same. There is a certain plastic look that everyone gets once they start going down that route.

H *I think, if you are going to get anything done, the golden rule is for God's sake don't touch your lips! They always look terrible and you're not kidding anyone, are you?*

F *Yuck! I just don't want that stuff injected into my face. Where does it go? And also if you've had it and then stop, then I think you look really, really rubbish and that scares me too, when you start depending on stuff. I want to go the natural route as much as I can.*

H *Yes, but when you do need a little help it is nice to know that it's there.*

F *What sort of help? I mean something like lipo is totally alien to me. I could never do that. The trick is to work out and eat well – otherwise it is just cheating. It is the easy way out and it is not good. I work out a few times a week. I like to do a six-kilometre run. It makes me feel better. Having it all sucked out wouldn't.*

Obviously if you do decide to do go down the route of the knife and the needle, then we agree you should be sure of a few things. The place you go to should be reputable, you should have researched your subject well and your expectations should not be too high. A new pair of boobs, a new nose or a smooth forehead are not going to change your life. If you talk to surgeons they say that those who expect radical changes from surgery, those who think the world will be a different place after they come round, are the ones who shouldn't be operated on in the first place. Just as a haircut doesn't lengthen your legs, give you a flat stomach and turn you into Gisele, so new lips and tits don't make you happy. Coming to terms with all the lumps and bumps and creases is a cheaper and healthier way to live. Then if you want a shiny, happy forehead, that's up to you!

HELP! AM I TURNING INTO MY MOTHER?

There are some things that even the most drastic forms of plastic surgery can't prevent. And no matter how hard you try, you just can't help it. You know the moment. You say something that sounds strangely familiar. It just trots off the tongue before you can stop yourself. Then you pass a shop window, glance across at a reflection you vaguely recognise. You pick up a catalogue at the dentist and actually flick through with interest. You begin to develop more than a fleeting curiosity in Tupperware. Or you find yourself strangely drawn to the comfy shoe section. And then it dawns on you – you're Mummamorphing. You are turning into your mum and there is nothing you can do about it. It can happen at any age and at any time. It is not dependent on martial status or having children – although they can speed up the process!

F *It is inevitable. No matter how much you fight it, it will happen. I have learnt things from my mum. She is an amazing woman. But I don't want to be her or turn into her. There are some things I can't help, though. I worry about being five minutes late; I always worry about being late. That's one of her pet hates. And I have just recently found myself doing that.*

H *You just can't stop it. You may as well accept it! I was never tidy or organised. I was a very scatty and airy-fairy type. And now I am a clean freak! I plump cushions the whole time. My mum used to plump them so much you couldn't actually sit on them and now I am the same. 'No, don't sit there, that sofa is just for looking at!' And now we hang out and say the same thing at the same time. But having said that, my mum is one amazing lady and if I do turn out like her, particularly in how she is as a mum, I'd be very happy!*

F *I hope to be just as good at juggling life as my mum. She worked three different jobs and looked after us kids and made it look easy. I do want to do stuff that she missed out on in life though. The world is a big and interesting place and she has stopped herself doing lots of things through fear. Fear of flying and trying new places, and I don't want to miss out on a thing.*

HOLLY AND HER MUM

HOLLY'S MUM

FEARNE'S MUM

my mum - my idol

The mumatron AKA Lin dressed ala 80's! Nice tights!

H   When I call my mother, it is like she has called me. She has a list of things she wants to say and I don't get a word in. I bet I end up doing that to my children.

F   My mother always arrives with a whole load of bits of paper that she has to give me, even before she has sat down. It is like some sort of ritual. If I give her a bag of stuff I have got together after a clear-out she always goes through it taking things out of the bag one by one and saying: 'You don't want this?' No, I say. That's why it's in the bag. 'But you don't want it?' No – that's why I put it in the bag. 'Why not?' She does it with every single thing. It drives me crazy.

H   You will definitely end up doing that! I can see it. But I tell you one thing, having a baby changes a few things. It makes you much more sympathetic to your mum. You realise that she went through the same things that I am going through with Harry. She must have felt the same things. It is weird. When I was pregnant she came over and wanted to do all my ironing. And I didn't want her to. But then, if it were the other round and my daughter was eight months pregnant, I would want to do the same, I suppose.

F   The thing is you want to prove that you are a grown-up and they still want you to be their little girl and therein lies the battle.

H   I am just starting to realise that I should let her do it. It doesn't really matter, does it? If anyone is having problems with their parents they should sit down and take ten minutes and think about it from their perspective. Maybe I just think that now that I am in this position?

F   They are usually only trying to do their best. They are human like we are.

CLOTHES, FROCKS AND TOGS - THE OUTER YOU

We are both obsessed with clothes. We love clothes. We talk about clothes. We think about clothes. We even have our own clothing lines, which we are very involved in and very proud of. In fact, there is nothing that delights us more than getting dressed up. Clothes can change your mood, boost your confidence and make you feel a whole lot better about yourself.

TO SPEND OR NOT TO SPEND

If you are feeling down, a bit of retail therapy can put a spring in your stride. We like to shop with the best of them. Embracing your inner Sarah Jessica Parker and burning some plastic can bring a smile to a girl's face. But we both think that retail need not cost the Earth. In fact, it is a whole lot better for you if it doesn't cost that much at all. Smart girls shop smart. Only the foolish and the flash cover themselves head to foot in labels. It's not cool and it's not clever and, most importantly, it doesn't look very nice.

F I love a bit of high street. It is so easy to look in a magazine and think, wow, she looks amazing, and go out and buy the outfit and put it on and look like a tit. You have to think about what suits you and what you like. I love high street plus a Mulberry bag. I love Mulberry bags more than anything in the world. That is my extravagance.

H Every girl loves shoes and handbags. But I really hate paying a huge amount of money for anything. And you don't really need to. The high street gets the stuff from the catwalk really quickly. You'd be mad to pay huge amounts for things.

F I also love a second-hand shop. I love rummaging and finding quirky odd things. My mum has given me loads of stuff from the seventies that I have mixed and matched.

That is easy for you to say. If you are shaped like Fearne you can probably go straight in somewhere and buy any old pair of jeans. But if you are shaped like me, you need to find a pair that fit properly and that is a little bit more difficult, so you might have to spend some money to get the right pair. You need a pair that hold you in and up and don't go baggy.

I always think about pounds-per-wear. If I feel guilty about how much something was, I work out cost per wear and don't feel so bad.

 I agree, although I never buy expensive sunglasses as I lose them all the time. I buy high street.

I agree. I never buy expensive sunglasses. I think it's uncool to look like you have tried too hard and spent thousands on your clothes. If you walk out of the house and look like you have spent hours getting ready, that is not good. Feel confident above everything but make it look effortless – that's the trick.

 It is important to wear clothes that don't wear you. You spend the whole day hitching things up or pulling things down. You have to feel comfortable.

I hate turning up and being overdressed. I feel like a tit.

 My style is much more formal. It is easier for me to be dressed up than to be casual, so I tend to look smarter than anyone else. When I was younger I used to find it difficult. Now I am older I don't mind so much. It is a confidence thing.

It is a question also of following the rules. Don't do legs and tits. Cover the top half if you are exposing the bottom half. Make a feature of one part of the body – make it about your waist, or legs, or your boobs, but not all at the same time. It is not attractive.

For me it is just not realistic to be dictated to by fashion. I can do my version of it but I can't do the whole thing. Like, for example, skinny jeans aren't great. I can't do them. I couldn't put them on and walk down the street. I'd look like a triangle. But if I did a dress and a belt over skinny jeans, then that's OK.

 In the States I did a show where they put me in a skin-tight dress that pushed my boobs up and I felt like a right idiot. I couldn't present properly. It was a disaster. I had no sense of humour and I couldn't work. I did it for the first month and then I put my foot down, which is something I hate doing. They let me put some more jewellery on and cover up and I was so much better. I felt like me again and it really made my work better. Clothes affect your mood. The shape, the colour – it all makes a difference. When I wake up I think about whether I am in a black mood, a grey mood or a colourful mood, and then I dress accordingly.

So you have your outfit. What do you put with it? Do your bag and shoes have to match? How many necklaces are too many? Or are you like Patsy in *Ab Fab* who once said, 'You can never have too many shoes, gloves and handbags.'

 Fearne can never have enough accessories. I have my one watch, my one necklace and my wedding ring and that's it. I wear the same stuff every day and I never change it. It is simple and it works and I don't have to think about it.

 They always say, take off the last thing you put on. I always say, put more on! I take all my rings off every night otherwise I would do myself some damage and then I put them all on again in the morning. I had three necklaces on today and I looked at myself in the car and thought, that's not enough. I feel naked without it all on. I am a real fidget. I need to play or fiddle with something all the time.

 I don't think your bag and shoes have to match but I do think you have to have matching bra and pants. It's my thing.

F *God, I only have two bras that fit me! I wear the same one for about three days, wash it, and by then the other one is dry enough for me to wear.*

H *Why don't you buy more of the ones that fit?*

F *Oh yes, I never thought of that!*

H *I am obsessed with good underwear. If you are wearing good underwear that is half the battle done for you. I clear my drawers out every six months or so and buy a whole load of new stuff. I keep the favourites. Some I never wear but I keep them because they have memories.*

F *Memories! You have underwear with memories!*

H *I have a red spotty Agent Provocateur pair of pants that I will never throw away.*

F *I don't want to know! That is already way too much information. I hate expensive pants because you have to hand-wash them, which is very annoying. I love Hanky Panky pants. One size fits all, they are from the States and I bulk-bought a whole load of them last time I was there. I don't want to wear anything else.*

H *I like wearing good underwear. It makes me carry myself better. I haven't got matching underwear on now and I know it!*

F *I understand wearing good underwear when you are first going out with someone, but six months later, who can be bothered?*

In our experience, men don't seem to like the same pants as we do! We have both in the past stocked up on date pants or some sort of sexy lingerie, only for the blokes we were with to either run scared, be totally turned off or not to remark on them at all. It appears that women are from La Senza and men are from Marks and Spencer!

H My husband likes those big pull-up pants that you wear under a dress. He thinks they are very sexy and fifties. He likes big pants.

F My last boyfriend hated thongs. But then he also hated big pants.

H I hate a thong. So uncomfortable. There's nothing worse.

F I don't think anyone likes them, really. They just pretend they do.

H Who buys them?

F Who knows?

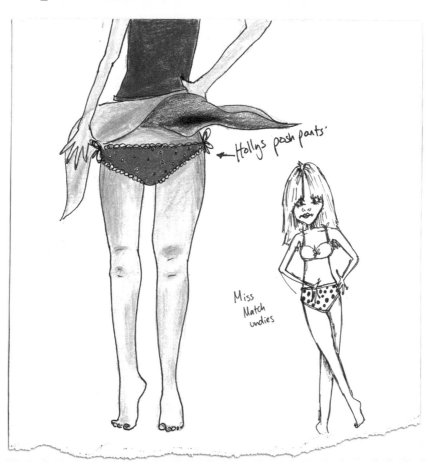

← Holly's posh pants

Miss Match undies

You've dealt with the outer you. Your bra and pants match. Your karma has been massaged along with your chakra and you've moisturised yourself from head to painted toenail while morphing slowly into your mum – the only thing left to think about is your actual inner you. Yourself. The older both of us have got, the more self-knowledge we have managed to accumulate – or so we hope. We hope we have learnt not to repeat the same mistakes, date the same men or drink the same virulent cocktail again that made us so ill the last time around. We hope we might have progressed, grown up even – just a tiny bit? But neither of us is actually holding our breath. We both know that learning from experience is harder than it looks. From the outside both of us appear to have it all, the career, the fun, the glamorous lifestyle, but it doesn't mean we don't have the same worries and fears as everyone else.

F *Sometimes I think I cling a bit too much to my teenage hopes, which worries me. There is a cool clique in showbiz London and I am really intimidated by them. It is like being back at school again and I keep having to remind myself that I am an adult, I have my mates, I don't need to hang with them to be happy. But it is hard to stop myself thinking, I should be cool, I am not cool enough. Who gives a shit? People might think I am rock 'n' roll but I am not. I make bloody cupcakes on a Friday night, even though I am wearing leather leggings to do it.*

H *What I am is a wife and mother, which is fantastic because it is what I always wanted. I have never been a girl who enjoyed being single. I have only been single for about six months of my life. But just because I am married doesn't mean that life has to be boring. I just have to work that bit harder at keeping it all together.*

Coming to terms with who you are and learning to live with yourself is one of the hardest and most important things to do.

H *I know I am never going to be a size 8. Never. Ever. So I have dealt with that! But I am also a bit compulsive. I get quite bogged down in the detail of things. I want everything to run smoothly so I am very obsessively organised. But the only problem is that I never reap the rewards of being organised because I am on to the next thing. One thing that having Harry has made me learn to do is to take a step back a bit. You have to let the pot sit in the sink; life just gets in the way.*

F *I really struggle with things like my self-image. Before it was very difficult because I wanted to be hip and out there, not eating fish fingers and chips with my mum. Now I love that and crave it.*

Knowing your faults and foibles, knowing yourself and trying to come to terms with your weaknesses, your demons even, and facing them head on, are things that both of us would love to be able to do.

F *I can't plan anything. It scares me to think about booking a holiday in a month's time. I can only live for the moment. I am not very good at thinking or planning ahead.*

H *The more decisions you have to make, the better you get at making them. You can train yourself to become good at these things. I always have quite a clear vision of what I want and I am quite decided when it comes to things. I don't regret them. Occasionally I say I wish I hadn't done something, but it is usually quite trivial stuff. And now I have a baby I am much more focused and much more organised.*

F *But I think that by making a decision I may shut off an opportunity. I like to keep all my options open. I also like the adventure of the unknown. I like to feel natural and unplanned, I like leaving things to fate. Having said that, I rarely regret the decisions I make.*

H *That's because you don't make any!*

F *That's true. You've got me there!*

We hope we've managed to persuade you that you time is not selfish time; it is kind of essential. Our philosophy is, if you look after yourself and respect yourself, then hopefully others will do the same. Don't obsess about what other people think of you, or about what other people think you should look like or be wearing. Be yourself. Embrace all your faults. Try to change the things you can change. Don't sweat the stuff you can't. And if all else fails, get yourself some matching underwear!

FEARNE AND HOLLY'S LISTS

5

FEARNE'S LIST

TOP 5 SHOPPING SECRETS

1 Portobello Road. The market on a Friday is the best.

2 Also one of my fave vintage shops is called Best Vintage, on Portobello Road. The girls in there always help me pick out fun new looks!

3 Melrose in LA. The vintage shops on Melrose are cheap, exciting and packed! I could browse around these shops for hours, spend very little and come back with so much original goodness!

4 The Old Cinema on Chiswick High Road. Another Aladdin's cave of wonder. From sixties furniture to fifties hats. I've picked up original eighties Rolling Stones posters, vintage dresses and French shabby-chic desks in here! I have been known to wander around this shop for hours. HEAVEN!

5 The Blue Bird on the King's Road. This is for super treats and special occasions. Gorgeous designer clothes, coffee table books and my favourite perfume is also sold here. There's also a wee café for coffee and chat after a shattering morning's shopping!

1 One of my fave red-carpet looks was a red jumpsuit I wore to the Brits one year. A lot of people said it looked like I was wearing PJs but I LOVED it. The colour was vibrant and it was so comfy!

2 I'm really into wearing long skirts at the moment. I'm going for Boho-grunge vibes all round. So a failsafe outfit is my fave long black skirt with a baggy jumper and Converse. Converse are the ultimate shoe!

3 I wore one of my own designs from Very to this year's NTAs, which was an exciting moment for me. Seeing one of my drawings come to life as an outfit was truly a dream come true. It was nerve-racking showcasing it at the awards but I seemed to get a good response.

ONE OF MY FAVOURITE DRESSES

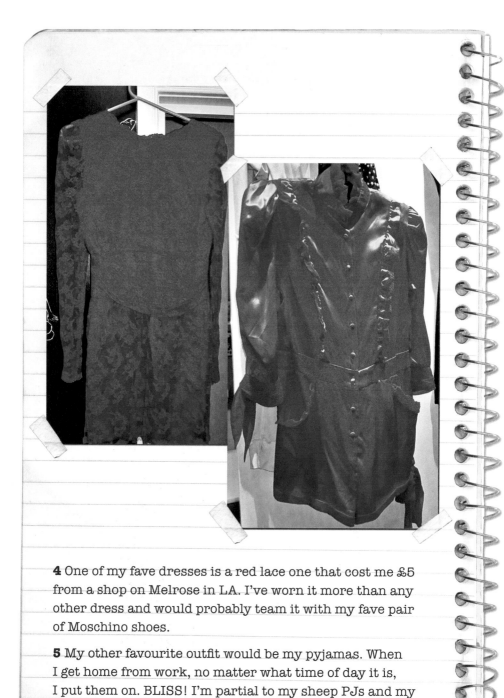

4 One of my fave dresses is a red lace one that cost me £5 from a shop on Melrose in LA. I've worn it more than any other dress and would probably team it with my fave pair of Moschino shoes.

5 My other favourite outfit would be my pyjamas. When I get home from work, no matter what time of day it is, I put them on. BLISS! I'm partial to my sheep PJs and my star-covered ones complete with granny slippers.

5 BEST HOLIDAY DESTINATIONS

1 Thailand! A little island off Phuket where I ate delicious food, swam in the warm sea and learnt about the lovely culture there.

2 Yosemite National Park for New Year was a cosy affair. Thick snow fell off the trees outside the hotel as I spent the whole time curled up by the fire reading a book with a hot choc in my hand. I MUST go back there soon!

3 Hawaii. It has always been a fantasy of mine to go there and it totally lived up to it. The food, the vast breathtaking beaches and the most incredible hikes to hidden waterfalls.

4 One of the funniest holidays I've ever had is when I was seventeen and my best school friend and I went to Zante in Greece. We fulfilled every cliché: i.e. drinking cocktails named after sexual acts, snogging holiday reps and getting burnt. Hilarious. Such good memories.

Me/t Ally AKA conholio in Greece! Drunk in awful 90's outfits!

5 Another momentous holiday was Majorca age fifteen where I met my first boyfriend. We walked past each other on the promenade and it was a bit like a movie. Waves crashing, music playing in my head and of course all in slow motion. We dated for years after and he's still a great friend now.

5 THINGS TO PACK ON HOLIDAY

1 Suntan lotion. As I get older this is a staple I lather it on in high factor.

2 Loads of flat shoes. I always end up wasting valuable packing space taking high shoes and never wear them. Don't bother.

3 Loads of bikinis. You don't want to waste chilling-out time washing manky saltwater ones.

4 LOADS of great sun-lounger books to get stuck into.

5 A camera. I love looking at old holiday photos and remembering great times!

5 WAYS TO RELAX

1 Painting is my favourite way to zone out. I go into a meditative state and can get lost for hours.

2 Reading is another way I can be transported into another world. A good book is hard to beat.

3 Squeezing as many of my mates around my kitchen table as I can. I get some cake in. We drink vast quantities of tea and chat for hours. Laughing is one of my favourite hobbies! Euphoric laughter!

4 Getting a massage. A rather clichéd form of relaxing but failsafe none-the-less.

5 Going to the cinema. A giant bag of pic'n'mix for my child-like sweet tooth and a great movie. A fantastic way of seeing life from someone else's perspective.

10 BEST RELAXING SONGS

1 Bon Iver, 'Skinny Love'. A delicious love song that is so good it makes my heart hurt a bit.

2 Slash (feat. Adam Levine), 'Gotten'. Any woman who has had a difficult relationship can relate to this one. Her beautiful tones send me into a physical melt.

3 Fleet Foxes, 'Blue Ridge Mountains'. This got me through many a painful moment climbing Mount Kilimanjaro.

4 Led Zeppelin, 'The Rain Song'. My favourite band in the world in their softest, most hushed tones.

5 Jeff Buckley, 'Lover, You Should've Come Over'. Some of the best lyrics ever written. The perfect Sunday song.

6 Laura Marling, 'Ghosts'. The most under-rated female vocalist in the UK.

7 Neko Case, 'Star Witness'.

8 Boston, 'More Than A Feeling'. Hilarious, I know, but brings back amazing memories from my youth.

9 Bob Dylan, 'Tangled Up In Blue'.

10 David Bowie, 'It Aint Easy'. One of the most powerful and amazing tunes ever.

FEARNE

TWO OF MY FAVORITE PAINTINGS THAT ONE DAY
WILL HOPEFULLY END UP IN AN EXHIBITION!
DAVID BOWIE ABOVE

PEACHES (ELECTRO MUSIC ARTIST)

1 Eat, Pray, Love by Elizabeth Gilbert. I wanted to go off travelling forever after this book.

2 Monster Love by Carol Topolski. One of the most gruesome books I've ever read. I couldn't put it down. I read it in about three days and was almost relieved to get to the end.

3 Kill Your Friends by John Niven. A fantastic book about the debauchery of the music A&R business back in the nineties. Again, totally gruesome, but a hilarious read! I felt bad for laughing but you can't help it.

4 Bright Shiny Morning by James Frey. Such a good, even representation of LA and its varied scene. Knowing the area well, I felt like I could hop there every night when I was reading this.

5 The Pursuit of Love by Nancy Mitford. A classic I think every girl should read. Especially if you are indeed a true, wholehearted romantic, like me.

5 BEAUTY TIPS

1 Always take your make-up off. Even if really drunk!

2 Whack on some red lippie if you're feeling blue. This always works for me and adds at least 20 per cent of happiness to my day.

3 Use moisturiser. Use too much moisturiser – we don't want to look like used tea bags when we are older.

4 Put conditioner on your hair and leave it in overnight. This will lead to amazing lustrous locks!

5 Put leave-in conditioner on your hair when you're on holiday in the sun as protection and to make it nice and soft when you go out in the evening.

Holly's List

TOP 5 SHOPPING SECRETS

1 'My Little Man' – that's me and my mum's name for a lovely chap who owns an antique shop on the Seven Dials roundabout in Brighton.

2 The Lanes in Brighton – great for a potter!

3 Very.co.uk.

4 Kitchen Shop, Barnes High Street – porn for foodies.

5 Christian Louboutin, Motcomb Street – the best shoes in the world.

TOP 5 BEST OUTFITS WORN

1 That white dress.

2 My first puffball skirt from Tammy Girl when I was nine.

3 Mum's original seventies ski suit (when skiing).

4 Red McQueen number as seen on show one of X Factor 2009.

5 A Vivienne Westwood dress I bought in a size 8 . . .
I know it would be one of my top five if only I could fit in it!

5 BEST HOLIDAY DESTINATIONS

1 Cocoa Island, Maldives.

2 Tuscany, Dan's mum's house.

3 Venice.

4 LA for fun.

5 The ice hotel in Sweden.

My painting of Vivienne Westwood done in 2007.

5 THINGS TO PACK ON HOLIDAY

1 Latest bonkbuster.

2 Ten pairs of heels I'll never wear.

3 Bobby Brown sun cream – pricey but smells lush.

4 My laptop so I can Skype my folks.

5 A new album so I can force it to become the holiday album.

5 WAYS TO RELAX

Bath, bed, massage, reading, music . . . shall I go on?!

10 BEST RELAXING SONGS

1 Mazzy Star, 'Fade into You'

2 Blur, 'To the End'

3 Elton John, 'Tiny Dancer'

4 Gomez, 'Tijuana Lady'

5 Beatles, 'Something'

6 Kate Nash, 'Birds'

7 Elliott Smith, 'In the Lost and Found'

8 Oasis, 'I'm Outta Time'

9 The Beach Boys, 'God Only Knows'

10 Turin Brakes, 'Fishing for a Dream'

5 FAVE BOOKS

1 Twilight Saga by Stephenie Meyer – I'm obsessed and totally in love with a young vampire.

2 Pride and Prejudice by Jane Austen – we all need a Mr Darcy.

3 Lord of the Flies by William Golding.

4 Harry and His Bucket Full of Dinosaurs
by Ian Whybrow – it's my Harry's fave.

5 Anything by Jackie Collins.

5 BEAUTY TIPS

1 You really, really should try to take your make-up off before bed.

2 Heat up eyelash curlers with a hairdryer before use.

3 When applying glittery eyeshadow, use sellotape to remove excess glitter from your cheeks.

4 Less is more, unless moisturising.

5 Drink more liquid. Sadly I mean water and not vino!

HOLLY WEARING TOO MUCH MAKE-UP!

And The Cherry
On The Cake?

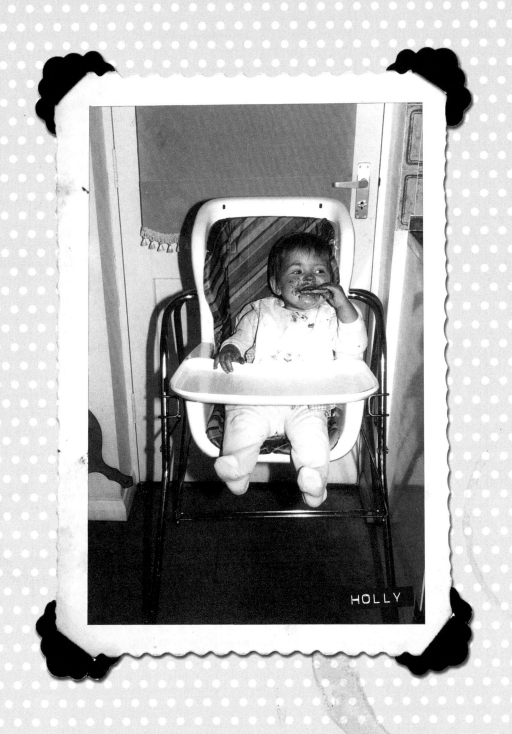

HOLLY

When all is said and done, your aim is to have your life in supposedly perfect balance. All your slices of cake should complement each other and not one of them should be out of proportion – your love life isn't dominating, your mates are not taking over, you are managing to spend some time thinking and dreaming on your own. Then your work/life balance is complete!

An impossible task, we know, and something we are working on ourselves on a daily basis. But we hope we have pointed you in a few good directions, stopped you from going down some dodgy roads and steered you away from emotional and career cul-de-sacs. Not that you, and we, won't make tons of mistakes along the way, because that is inevitable and unavoidable, but the trick is to learn from them. Don't be your own worst enemy. Break the cycle and change the way you live your life. Or at least, that is what we are trying to do!

And when you have the perfect cake, round and fat and delicious, beautifully iced and ready to sink your teeth into – what would be the cherry to put on top? The thing that made it all worthwhile? The one moment that would make you clench your fist and say: 'Yes!' A house? A husband? Babies? An Oscar? A number-one record? The Pulitzer Prize? A picnic in the park with a big gang of friends? Climbing a mountain? A sunset stroll along the beach?

F *This is so hard to pin down. In a long-term way it would be to have a family and a house by the sea where I could paint and have millions of cats and my kids running about. Long walks by the sea and good memories of the debauched crazy London life I used to lead. On a more flippant note, it would be to have a cup of tea with Jimmy Page and Robert Plant and to own an original Jack Vettriano painting. That would truly be the juiciest cherry available!*

H *I think being happy where you are, with what you have got is so important. Being happy at this precise moment, enjoying the moment and not wanting and not longing and not hankering after something else is a very powerful thing. Knowing and recognising when you are happy and holding on to it is the best cherry you can have on any cake.*

And it is at moments like these that you remember quite how lucky you are and quite what a fantastic best mate you have.

F *Mine and Holly's friendship is special because we have grown together. We have been at each other's sides as we've waded through a sometimes confusing and harsh working environment. We have grown up so much in our own fields, and have been able to be there for each other every step of the way. Congratulating each other on the highs, scooping each other back up after the lows and listening to each other's joys and frustrations. We weirdly got our new jobs, Holly on* This Morning, *and me, my Radio 1 show, on the same day! We secretly told each other first and then squealed a lot down the telephone! We have seen each other grow in relationships, some failed (mainly me) and some blossoming. I've watched Holly turn into* a wonderful mother and wife and seen her grow in so many other ways. Our friendship is ever changing but the foundations remain the same. We have been able to achieve some wonderful things together with our clothing ranges, TV shows and now this book. I think we are so different but I hope the many different types of fabulous women out there can relate to each of us. Together we are united. Two is more powerful than one. And we are friends for life, no matter what surprises life chooses to throw at us. One day to prove my love of Holly I'm going to climb a lamp post in LA and steal the street sign that bears the word 'Willoughby' and present it to her as a gift. I would get arrested for that girl.

H Two is most definitely better than one. This big bad world can be a lonely place if you're trapped with your own thoughts and even your own wardrobe. Fearne and I have been through a lot together and have the emotional scars and laughter lines to prove it. We've reached a great place in our friendship – it's almost like a good marriage minus the wet towels on the bathroom floor! We don't need to explain or justify ourselves to one another any more, we're done with trying to impress or keep up, we are who we are, and love each other truthfully. God help the man, woman or animal who crosses Fearne as they will have the wrath of Hurricane Holly to deal with!

To try to explain what Fearne is like as a friend is to try to explain the way you feel when you're around her. You know what it's like when winter is coming to an end: it's February, Christmas is over, your skin is the palest shade of grey and you're still trying to lose the extra pounds you gained over the festive period. Then one day you're outside in a whole world of grey and nothing and you see the first daffodil of spring. That emotion you feel right there is what it's like to hang out with Fearne. In the industry we work in there is a lot of grey . . . and she is the brightest of yellows.

FEARNE'S THANKYOUS

F Thanks to Imogen Edwards-Jones who chatted, listened and captured exactly what I think about love and life – a new wonderful friend made in the process. Thanks to the team at Vermilion for giving Holly and I the opportunity to get this book out to many girls who are trying to work out what it's all about, just like me.

Thanks to my mum, Linda, who has always given me the freedom to love and live as freely and passionately as I like. Thanks for putting up with me bringing all sorts of men into your life and moaning quite a lot. Mums always know best.

Thanks to my dad, the man who has set the standard as to what a gent and husband should be. Never raising his voice or losing his cool in any situation. The best man on Earth.

Thanks to my little brother for putting up with a loudmouth older sister who has probably put him off women for life.

Thanks to Alison at James Grant for being superwoman. Someone who not only keeps my life and chaos in order, but who also remains a solid and understanding friend.

Thanks to Holly, Cherise, Lolly, Hayley, Becky, Ally, Sarah, Sinead, JJ, Lucy and India for being the best girls a girl could have. Always there to make me laugh, forget and dance. I feel so lucky to have met these wonderful people and to call them true friends.

Also thanks to Kye, Reggie, Jake and Bundy. Honorary girls who understand women as much as a boy ever could. Thanks to Biba, Shannon, Jess, Ben and Katie. How lucky I am to be great mates with my cousins. People who I didn't choose to have in my life but am so glad are.

Thanks to Lauren Chambers and Ellis Clarke: two little girls who lost their own battles on this Earth far too early but who taught me a lifetime's worth of love and determination in such a short time.

I was going to thank all my ex-boyfriends for teaching me what love, lust and loss is all about but I'm not sure some of them deserve it! Ha!

Finally thanks to you for reading this book. Whether you're looking for advice, a laugh or just a mate, I hope you have found it here.

Love and peace,

H Mum – you are without doubt the perfect combination of beauty, grace and patience all wrapped up in motherly love and tied with a ribbon of cuddles. You are my inspiration. Dad – thank you for filling my head with the sound of laughter, for being so proud of your girls you could burst, for having enthusiasm for everything you do and for protecting and guiding me every step of the way. Kelly – I still look up to you and admire you every day, my little Miss October, my sister and my other best friend. Dan – thank you for being you, for being a great Dad, for loving me unquestionably and for letting me love you entirely, I'm blessed to have you in my life. Harry – when you grow older this may help you to understand the labyrinth of a girl's mind. Be less like me, and more like your father – he's a great man. I love you. James Grant Media, in particular John Knight – he literally is my knight in shining lycra! Thanks to Imogen Edwards-Jones, who listened to all our endless rambling and suffered in silence at my ridiculously bad emailing skills.

having a laugh with Mulhern

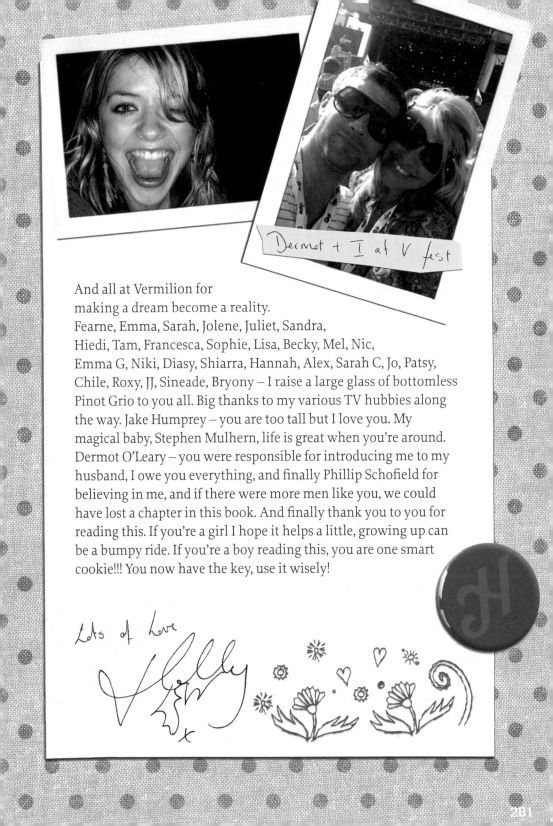

Dermot + I at V fest

And all at Vermilion for
making a dream become a reality.
Fearne, Emma, Sarah, Jolene, Juliet, Sandra,
Hiedi, Tam, Francesca, Sophie, Lisa, Becky, Mel, Nic,
Emma G, Niki, Diasy, Shiarra, Hannah, Alex, Sarah C, Jo, Patsy,
Chile, Roxy, JJ, Sineade, Bryony – I raise a large glass of bottomless
Pinot Grio to you all. Big thanks to my various TV hubbies along
the way. Jake Humprey – you are too tall but I love you. My
magical baby, Stephen Mulhern, life is great when you're around.
Dermot O'Leary – you were responsible for introducing me to my
husband, I owe you everything, and finally Phillip Schofield for
believing in me, and if there were more men like you, we could
have lost a chapter in this book. And finally thank you to you for
reading this. If you're a girl I hope it helps a little, growing up can
be a bumpy ride. If you're a boy reading this, you are one smart
cookie!!! You now have the key, use it wisely!

Lots of Love

x

INDEX

PICTURE CREDITS